SOUND AND LIGHT

PHYSICS IN ACTION

Atomic and Nuclear Physics

Electricity and Magnetism

Energy

Forces and Motion

Heat and Thermodynamics

The Nature of Matter

Planets, Stars, and Galaxies

Processes That Shape the Earth

Sound and Light

SOUND AND LIGHT

Heather E. Hillesheim

CHELSEA HOUSE
An Infobase Learning Company

To my physics students

SOUND AND LIGHT

Chelsea House
An imprint of Infobase Learning
132 West 31st Street
New York NY 10001

Library of Congress Cataloging-in-Publication Data
Hillesheim, Heather.
  Electricity and magnetism / author, Heather Hillesheim.
    p. cm. — (Physics in action)
  Includes bibliographical references and index.
  ISBN 978-1-61753-098-2
  1. Electricity. 2. Magnetism. I. Title.
  QC522.H55 2012
  537—dc23
                        2011022955

Chelsea House books are available at special discounts when purchased in bulk quantities for businesses, associations, institutions, or sales promotions. Please call our Special Sales Department in New York at (212) 967–8800 or (800) 322–8755.

You can find Chelsea House on the World Wide Web at
http://www.infobaselearning.com

Text design by James Scotto-Lavino
Composition by Kerry Casey
Illustrations by Dale Williams
Photo research by Elizabeth H. Oakes
Cover printed by Yurchak Printing, Landisville, Pa.
Book printed and bound by Yurchak Printing, Landisville, Pa.
Date printed: March 2012
Printed in the United States of America

10 9 8 7 6 5 4 3 2 1

This book is printed on acid-free paper.

CONTENTS

ACKNOWLEDGMENTS

Life takes strange turns. I never thought I would ever write a book, much less one about physics. Many people influenced those turns and helped me along this path, and I would like to thank them. First, thank you to my parents, both fantastic teachers, who instilled in me a love of learning just for the sake of gaining new knowledge. I would also like to thank Stefanie Stinchcomb who gave me the chance to try teaching physics—despite my degree in chemistry—just because I thought it would be interesting. It helped me find that physics is my favorite subject, and I will always be thankful for the opportunity. I also need to thank Elaine Wood and Pam Walker for suggesting me when asked about a "physics person." I never would have gotten this opportunity otherwise. A huge thanks goes to my editor, Frank Darmstadt, for his extreme patience. From a daily email or two (or ten honestly), to helping me learn what an em dash is and when to use it, Frank was patient with my mistakes and always respectful of my knowledge. This project would not even exist without you: thank you so much.

I also need to thank my husband, Daniel, for advice on my research (even if sometimes he got overly technical) and patience when I neglected things around the house to get just a little more written. Thanks go as well to my daughter, Keely, for letting me squeeze in a few more minutes of writing by entertaining herself once in awhile. Thanks also go to Megan and Tim, two fantastic friends, for reminding me that your past helps determine who you are today and for being there through so much of mine. Final thanks go to my sister, Julie, who always knows when I need a break.

OVERVIEW

Sound and light are two fundamental aspects of experiencing life. Life without being able to hear or see anything is hard to imagine. On the surface, sound and light seem very different. The blast of a car horn and the beam of a flashlight do not seem similar; however, both are forms of energy carried by waves, and they exhibit some of the same properties. Sound waves can be reflected off a surface like in an echo. Light can also be reflected such as when people see themselves in a mirror. Although light and sound waves travel in slightly different ways, vibration is always the source of the motion. The energy of the sound wave vibrates the molecules of the medium through which the sound is traveling, and the electric and magnetic fields in a light wave vibrate.

Sound and Light discusses both of these types of waves—from how they are generated to how they interact with the world around them. This field of physics is one of the most applicable to a person's everyday life. Knowledge about light and sound helps to answer frequently asked questions such as why the ocean is blue and why the siren on an ambulance seems to change pitch as it drives past.

Chapter 1 discusses the vibrations that cause waves and the three types of waves—transverse waves, longitudinal waves, and surface waves—that can be formed. The chapter also explores the difference between mechanical waves and electromagnetic waves and describes the parts of a wave. Finally, chapter 1 explains how waves are measured in terms of wavelength, frequency, period, and velocity.

Chapter 2 explains how sound waves travel and describes the different ways in which sound interacts with the matter around it. The chapter discusses topics such as what makes a barrier soundproof and explains the science behind the use of acoustics to produce good sound in a concert hall. Chapter 2 concludes by explaining the Doppler effect, which is a very important component of how sound waves behave in our daily lives. People experience this effect, for example, when an ambulance drives by them and in certain medical tests, including ultrasounds and echocardiograms.

Chapter 3 describes the other type of wave that this book dis-cusses—light. The chapter describes the entire electromagnetic spectrum from radio waves to visible light and finally to gamma rays. The chapter also mentions how each of these types of light waves and natural sources are used and explains the production and travel of electromagnetic waves and compares these processes to sound waves.

Chapter 4 turns its attention to just the visible portion of the electromagnetic spectrum—the source of all the color that can be seen. The chapter explains the order of the colors in a rainbow in terms of energy and wavelength and presents reasons behind phenomena, such as why a leaf looks green and why the sky looks blue. The chapter ends with a discussion of additive and subtrac-tive colors. Surprisingly, primary colors are different depending on whether they are additive or subtractive colors. One type of color occurs when colored lights add together (additive colors), and the other type occurs when dyes absorb different colors of light (subtractive colors).

Chapter 5 uses the law of reflection to explain why a clear image can be seen in surfaces that are smooth, like glass, but not in rough surfaces. This chapter continues by describing the three types of mirrors: plane mirrors, convex mirrors, and concave mir-rors. It goes on to explain how to draw a ray diagram for each type of mirror. These diagrams help to determine the type of image formed. Images can be real or virtual, meaning that the light rays can really cross where the image forms or only appear to cross. Images can also be upright or inverted and reduced or magnified. Finally, the chapter explains some everyday uses of mirrors, such as those in reflecting telescopes and cameras.

Chapter 6 provides a very similar discussion about lenses. The chapter uses Snell's law to explain why, and by how much, light bends as it passes through a new substance. This law can be used to explain why items at the bottom of a pool are not where they appear to be when someone reaches into the water to grab them. The chapter discusses the two types of lenses—convex and con-cave—along with their ray diagrams, and the images that they form. The uses of lenses in objects like eyeglasses and refracting telescopes are the final topic in this chapter.

Chapter 7 gives details on two more ways in which waves interact with the matter around them and with each other, interference and diffraction. These two interactions occur with both light waves and sound waves. Interference occurs when two waves collide and can be either constructive interference, which produces a larger wave after collision, or destructive interference, which produces a smaller wave after collision. The chapter states that diffraction occurs when waves bend through an opening or around an obstacle and explains why it happens. It goes on to discuss the ways in which diffraction is used and when it is seen, such as

The narrow grooves covering the back of a CD create a diffraction grating. The bending of the light waves through and around the grating creates rainbows of color. (Courtesy of Peter Brock)

when a person can see the rainbow of colors on the back of a CD. The last topic of this chapter is standing waves. A standing wave occurs when the wave appears to hold a constant position; these types of waves are usually produced by the interference of two identical waves moving in opposite directions. Musical instruments frequently use standing waves to produce a rich, full sound.

Light and sound play an important role in people's lives—from the music that they play to the sights that they see. Seldom does a person stop to question why light and sound waves behave a certain way. However, this knowledge is behind much of modern technology, for example, quality television screens, state-of-the-art medical testing, ideal home sound systems, and much more.

Vibrations and Types of Waves

Since vibrations create waves, chapter 1 starts with a discussion of the different vibrations that create different types of waves. Vibrations in different directions cause a wave to move differently. This chapter introduces the terms for different parts of waves and explains how waves are measured and quantitatively described. Much of the material here will be used as a foundation for understanding the material presented in later chapters of this book.

VIBRATIONS

Waves transport energy from one place to another through vibrations. **Electromagnetic waves** do not require a substance, or **medium**, to travel through, which is why light rays from the Sun can travel through the vacuum of space. In an electromagnetic wave, an electric field and a magnetic field both vibrate and allow the energy to travel. Electromagnetic waves are commonly called *light waves*, even though they include much more than the visible colors of light. Chapter 3 will discuss the electromagnetic spectrum in greater detail.

In **mechanical waves**, vibrations occur in the medium through which the wave is traveling. For example, when a person shakes a rope in order to send a wave down its length, the particles of the rope vibrate, or move back and forth, in order to transmit the energy of the wave. As each section of rope moves up or down, it pulls the adjoining section along with it and transfers energy. Some of the transferred energy is lost due to **friction**, such as the air resistance between the rope and the air around it, but most of the energy is transmitted. With a long enough rope, eventually all the energy would be lost, and the wave would cease to travel. It is important to realize that although the energy travels from one end of the medium to the other, the actual medium particles do not travel very far. They merely vibrate back and forth within a small area.

TYPES OF WAVES AND THEIR PARTS

There are three common types of mechanical waves: **transverse waves**, **longitudinal waves**, and **surface waves**. In a transverse wave, the particles of the medium vibrate perpendicularly to the direction in which the wave is traveling. Some examples of transverse waves include a wave created by shaking a rope, the "wave" done at sporting events, and the seismic waves that cause earthquakes. The peak of a transverse wave is called a **crest**, and the low point is called a **trough**. The distance (in meters) from one crest to another is called a **wavelength**. This distance is useful because it gives the length of one repeating unit of a transverse wave—one crest plus one trough. The more energy a transverse wave carries the further the crests and troughs are displaced from the original resting position. This displacement is called the **amplitude** of the wave. A transverse wave that carries more energy will have higher crests and lower troughs than another transverse wave that carries less energy.

Longitudinal waves are the second type of mechanical wave. The particles in these types of waves vibrate in the same direction in which the wave is traveling. Sound is the most common type of longitudinal wave, but a sound wave is hard to visualize. Picture

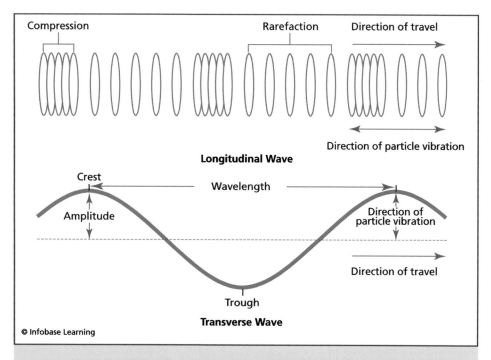

The particles in a transverse wave vibrate perpendicularly to the direction in which the wave travels while the particles in a longitudinal wave vibrate parallel to the direction in which the wave travels.

a "slinky" toy stretched out along a floor. A person can create a longitudinal wave by gently pushing (adding energy) one end of the slinky to send a "pulse" along its length. These waves transmit energy along the length of the wave as the particles move closer together and "push" the particles next in line; this action causes the pushed particles to bunch up while the first particles spread out.

Longitudinal waves have areas called **compressions** in which the particles of the medium are tightly pushed together. In between the compressions are areas called **rarefactions** in which the particles are stretched further apart. Compressions are analogous to the crests of transverse waves, and rarefactions are analogous to troughs. Since there is no perpendicular displacement, there is no easily visualized way to measure the amplitude of a longitudinal wave, although it can be measured in some situations. In a sound wave, the compressions are areas in which the air particles are closer together, causing higher pressure. In addition, rarefactions are areas of lower pressures than the air was previously at before the wave passed through. A sketch of a transverse wave can be created by graphing the change in pressure over the time elapsed. Measuring the amplitude of this graphed wave shows how far the pressure moves from the original pressure and allows one to calculate the amplitude of the longitudinal wave.

Surface waves are a combination of the previous two types of mechanical waves. If a beach ball is floating on the ocean as a wave moves underneath it, the ball first moves toward the wave and then up the wave's crest. The ball then rides the crest forward and finally comes back down. The particles of water in a surface wave move both with the wave's motion and perpendicular to it to create a circular pattern. Surface waves cannot be classified as either a transverse or a longitudinal wave because they have aspects of both types of waves and are therefore considered a separate type of mechanical wave.

Thus far, only mechanical waves have been discussed in terms of types of waves because all electromagnetic waves travel in the same manner. The vibration of an electric field creates a magnetic field; this process causes the electromagnetic wave to travel. Both of these fields exist as transverse waves. Thus, electromagnetic waves are actually two transverse waves traveling perpendicularly to each other.

MEASURING A WAVE

Not all waves of the same type are identical. For example, light can differ in color or exist in forms that are not visible to the naked eye, such as ultraviolet (UV) rays. A sound can be high pitched, a soft whisper, or a loud shout. Measurements must be taken to quantify the differences in these waves. The two most frequently used measurements of a wave are its wavelength and

Speed versus Velocity

Are speed and velocity the same thing? The answer to this question is *sometimes*. Speed is how quickly an object covers a distance; it can be calculated by dividing the distance traveled by the time it took to travel that distance. Velocity tells an object's speed and the direction in which it is moving. This distinction is important because an object can be moving forward, backward, sideways, or anything in between. For example, if a car is moving 52 feet per second (16 m per second) north and if a second car is moving 52 feet per second (16 m per second) south, both cars would have the same speed but not the same velocity. The difference in velocity would be shown either by including the north and south directions or by choosing a direction to be positive and showing the opposite direction with a negative sign in front of the number. For example, if north is designated the positive direction then the first car would be moving at +52 feet per second (+16 meters per second), while the second car has a velocity of -52 feet per second (-16 meters per second). With light and sound waves, speed and velocity can be used interchangeably because waves only move one direction—forward.

its **frequency**. The wavelength is a measurement of the length of a full cycle of a wave, one crest and one trough, or one compression and one rarefaction. Wavelength is always measured in meters; however, the number for waves with very small wavelengths, such as light, is usually written in nanometers. A nanometer is equal to 3.3×10^{-9} feet (1×10^{-9} m).

Frequency is the number of wavelengths that pass through a given point in 1 second—it is measured in the units of hertz (Hz), which means cycles per second (for example, 1 Hz is one cycle per second). Therefore, a frequency of 345 Hz means that 345 wavelengths pass any stationary point per second. Frequency and wavelength are inversely proportional to each other; there-

Calculating the Speeds of Sound and Light

The military has a strong interest in the accurate measurements of the speed of sound because these measurements help pinpoint the location of enemy artillery. An early method used to measure the speed of sound involved firing a cannon and then timing how long it took the sound of the blast to travel a specific distance. William Derham (1657–1735), an English vicar with an interest in science, made the first reasonably accurate measurement of the speed of sound in the early 18th century. Derham used a telescope set in the steeple of a church to note the plume of smoke when a cannon or gun was fired several miles away and timed how long it

Galileo tried to calculate the speed of light with a method more appropriate for use in calculating the speed of sound. (Courtesy of Wikimedia)

fore, as one increases the other must decrease. A high wavelength indicates that the wave is very wide and spread apart, whereas a high frequency indicates that the waves are close together to enable more waves to pass each second. In terms of sound waves, frequency is interpreted as **pitch**. A high-frequency sound wave is heard as a high-pitched sound, whereas low frequency is heard as a low-pitched sound. The **period** of a wave is the time that it takes for one full wavelength to pass a stationary point. Period is measured in seconds and is equal to the reciprocal of the frequency. For example, a sound wave with a frequency 440 Hz has a period took for the sound to reach him. This method was not perfectly accurate because of the effects of wind, temperature, and humidity on the speed of sound and because of inaccuracies in early timing devices, but it did provide a good starting point and was fairly accurate for most needs.

The speed of light proved much more difficult to measure as Galileo Galilei (1564–1642), the Italian astronomer and physicist, found in 1600. He designed an experiment in which an assistant with a lantern with shutters stood on the top of one hill while a second person stood at the top of another hill. Both people had synchronized watches, and the first person opened the lantern at previously specified times. The second person recorded how long it took him to see the light at each specified time. Unfortunately, Galileo found that when he doubled the distance between the two people, the time recorded was almost the same. He was measuring the reaction time of the person taking the measurements because the light traveled too fast to be measured at that distance. The first true measurement of the speed of light did not come until 1676 when the Danish astronomer Ole Rømer (1644–1710) used the eclipses of Jupiter with its moons to calculate the value. The speed of light is so great, that distances between two objects must be astronomical in order to provide enough recordable travel time.

of 0.00227 s—meaning that it takes that long for one wavelength to pass a specific point.

A final important measurement of a wave is its **velocity** or speed. Velocity is typically measured in meters per second. It can be calculated in one of two ways. First, in classical mechanics, velocity is defined as the distance traveled divided by the time it took, $v = d/t$. Wave speed can be measured this way as well. Suppose a man yells while standing in a canyon 492 feet (150 m) from the wall of the canyon. If it takes 0.87 seconds for the sound of his echo to return, he can calculate the speed of his voice. The man would divide the total distance that the sound traveled, 984 feet (300 m) (492 feet [150 m] to the wall and then 492 feet [150 m] back to him), by the time it took for the sound to travel 984 feet (300 m), 0.87 seconds. The velocity of that man's voice would be 1,132 feet per second (345 m per second). This method works fairly well with relatively slow moving waves; however, to calculate extremely fast moving waves, such as light, one must either use extremely large distances or must measure very tiny amounts of elapsed time.

The second method of calculating the speed of a wave involves its relationship with frequency and wavelength. The applicable equation states that the velocity of a wave is equal to its wavelength times its frequency: $v = \lambda \; x \; f$. Suppose a person rhythmically shakes a rope in order to send waves down its length. The waves have a wavelength of 2.5 feet (0.75 m) and four wavelengths pass a set point each second. The velocity of these waves can be calculated by multiplying the wavelength times the frequency, 2.5 feet (0.75 m) times 4 Hz. The speed of these waves is 10 feet per second (3 m per second).

SUMMARY

Vibrations are the source of all wave movement, whether the wave is mechanical and is traveling through some type of material or whether the wave is an electromagnetic wave and is traveling through the empty void of space. These vibrations allow a wave to carry energy from one point to another. Mechanical waves are classified into one of three types of waves, depending on which way the medium particles are vibrating. Medium particles vibrating perpendicularly to the direction in which the wave is traveling form a transverse wave. Transverse waves have crests (high points) and troughs (low points). The amplitude of a transverse wave is a measurement of how far the medium is displaced by the vibration and is an indicator of the amount of energy traveling along the wave.

Medium particles traveling in the same direction as the wave motion form a longitudinal wave. Longitudinal waves have areas called *compressions* in which the medium particles are close together and areas called *rarefactions* in which the particles are further apart. Both types of waves can be measured in terms of wavelength—the length of one repeating cycle—and frequency. The frequency is the number of waves that pass a point in 1 second. Measurements of a wave's speed are also important when trying to quantitatively describe a wave. Surface waves are the final type of waves; these waves travel in a circular manner and have properties of both transverse and longitudinal waves.

All of this information is vital to the understanding of light and sound waves. It also helps explain why all colors and all sounds are not the same and gives one a way to describe how these waves are different. The basic information on all waves provided in chapter 1 is necessary to understand how waves interact with each other.

2

Sound

Sound is a fundamental aspect of most people's lives and the focus of chapter 2. The chapter covers the production of sound first, from general ideas about how sound propagates to specifics about how people produce sound. It next covers the ways that sound can be influenced to reduce noise or to make the sounds from a stage travel well. The chapter continues with a discussion on how the Doppler effect influences sound whenever either the source, or listener, is moving. Finally, it describes and explains the many uses of sound in our modern world.

PRODUCING SOUND

To produce a sound wave, energy must be transferred to the particles of the medium through which the sound will travel. If a sound is traveling through air, the air particles at the source of the sound become energetic and begin to vibrate. As these particles vibrate, they compress together and form the compression of the sound wave. The vibrating air particles come into contact with nearby particles and cause them to vibrate as energy is transferred. As the first molecules lose energy and begin to stop moving, they spread out and form the rarefaction of the sound wave. Sound travels in all directions away from the source, not just in a straight line. The compressed section of air molecules appears to travel along the air molecules in a circular fashion away from the source, although in reality the air molecules themselves only move a small distance. The energy is traveling from the source of the sound to the object receiving the sound.

Guitars produce sound through the vibration of their strings. The motion of the strings causes the air molecules to vibrate and create a sound wave. Although the term *vocal cords* seems to suggest that the human voice is produced by a similar type of vibration, it is actually produced by the opening and closing of these vocal cords—now more commonly called *vocal folds*. Vocal folds are flaps of tissue within the larynx that lay over the top of the trachea or windpipe. The muscles of the larynx bring these folds close together in preparation for speaking. As air is pushed out of the lungs and up the windpipe, pressure builds up below the vocal folds. Once the pressure becomes high enough, it forces the folds to open enough for a puff of high-pressure air to escape, leaving behind an area of low-pressure air that allows the vocal folds to close again. The pressure soon builds up again underneath the vocal folds and leads to the escape of another puff of air. These cycles of high and low pressure create the sound wave. Muscles in the larynx tighten and move the folds to change the pitch and tone of the sound produced. The cheeks, tongue, and lips help modify the sound to produce specific letters and words.

The more energy used to cause the vibrations, the greater the change in pressure and the louder the sound produced. The loudness of sound is measured in **decibels**, which is measured on a logarithmic scale. Decibels measure the ratio of the air pressure of a sound versus a reference level. The lowest limit of sound audible to a human is defined as 0 decibels (dB), and all other measurements use this as a reference level. Typically, the smallest change in sound pressure, or volume, that is detectable by the human ear is 1 dB. A decibel is equal to one-tenth of a bel—the base unit for

How Speakers Work

Electromagnetism is a field of physics that explores the relationship between electricity and magnetism. In 1820, Hans Christian Ørsted (1777–1851), the Danish physicist, noticed a compass being deflected as it was

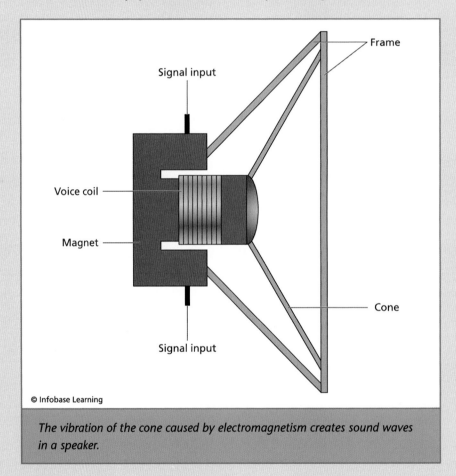

Signal input

Frame

Voice coil

Magnet

Cone

Signal input

© Infobase Learning

The vibration of the cone caused by electromagnetism creates sound waves in a speaker.

the measurement of sound intensity—but human ears are so sensitive to changes in pressure that even small changes are noticeable; therefore, bel units are rarely used. Decibels were originally brought near a wire with electricity flowing through it. He soon discovered that any straight wire carrying a current created a circular magnetic field around the wire. If the wire is wound up into a tight coil, all of the magnetic fields of each coil of the wire line up and strengthen each other, creating an electromagnet. Electromagnets and their interactions with other permanent magnets are the basis of many of today's electronic devices.

Speakers are one of the most common sources of sound today. Inside every speaker is a cone that is usually made of paper or plastic. The base of the cone is wrapped in a coil of wire called the *voice coil*. A permanent magnet surrounds this coil. As electricity is run through the voice coil it becomes an electromagnet with a north pole and a south pole, just like all other magnets. The electromagnet is either repelled or attracted by the permanent magnet that surrounds it, depending on the orientation of the electromagnet's poles. This repulsion or attraction causes the cone to either push forward or pull back. A forward motion causes air particles to be pressed together, creating a compression. As the cone moves backward, a rarefaction is formed as the air particles become more spread out and less pressurized. The electrical current going to the voice coil can reverse its direction and thus change the orientation of the poles of the electromagnet; this process causes the cone to move in the opposite direction. Changing how fast the cone moves back and forth alters the frequency and pitch of the sound wave formed. Changes in the current can cause the repulsion and attraction to be stronger or weaker. This changing vibration of the cone is what causes the sound produced by speakers. As technology has allowed the permanent magnets in a speaker to become smaller, speakers themselves have gone down in size. Even the speakers in something as small as a cell phone work in this same manner.

used to measure the change in volume in telephone circuits and were named after Alexander Graham Bell (1847–1922), the Scottish scientist who invented the telephone.

Sound is a mechanical wave and does require a medium through which to travel, but that medium does not have to be a gas. In fact, sound travels slower in a gas than it does in a solid. The energy of a sound wave is transferred from one particle to another when the particles are in contact. The particles in a solid are much closer together and more tightly packed than the particles in a gas. The close contact between particles in a solid allows for the energy of a sound wave to be transferred more quickly from one particle to another. However, certain materials do have specific properties that help absorb the energy of sound waves and dampen the sound. These kinds of materials are often used for soundproofing.

SOUNDPROOFING AND ACOUSTICS

When sound is not welcome in a given situation, soundproofing is necessary to decrease the amount of sound waves that reach that location. There are several approaches to reducing sound waves, such as simply increasing the distance between the source and the receiver of the sound, placing objects between the source and receiver to help block some of the sound waves, and using sound damping materials such as baffles that absorb and change the sound. Many types of soundproofing use a combination of approaches. For example, people with homes located near large roadways depend on noise barriers to reduce the road sounds that reach their homes. These noise barriers serve to block noise from the road and are typically made of dense, tightly packed material. Some sound is transmitted through the wall, although it has typically lost a great deal of energy and will be distorted. In addition, some sound will also travel over the wall and down to the receiver. Special attention must be paid to preventing any gaps or holes in the wall because this greatly reduces the effectiveness. Noise barriers typically produce a 5- to 10-dB reduction in the noise that reaches the homes.

Soundproofing is used in many other ways. Curtains in a home help to reduce the sound transmitted through windows into the house. Mufflers on cars help to reduce the noise an en-

The fabric on the walls of this movie theater helps to prevent unwanted echoes and to improve acoustics. (Courtesy of Wikimedia)

gine produces. The walls of a recording studio must be carefully soundproofed to prevent outside noises from entering by adding sound-absorbing materials to the outsides and insides of the walls. Sound-absorbing materials are usually very dense but porous materials, such as polyurethane foam, that absorb sound by converting the energy from the sound wave into heat. This energy conversion occurs when the vibrating air molecules try to vibrate into the material and lose their energy through friction between the air molecules and the material. In movie theaters, the walls are frequently draped with fabric to help absorb the sound and to reduce echoes, as shown in the above figure. This fabric not only improves the sound within that theater but also helps to reduce the transmission of sounds between neighboring theaters.

At times, sound waves need to be controlled, for example, in a concert hall or auditorium. The continuation of a sound so that it reaches the back of the space and seems full and lively is desirable in these cases. This type of sound control is usually done by increasing **reverberation**—the total sum of all of the reflected sound waves from the surfaces within a space. Some echoes are wanted as they propagate the sound and increase its fullness; however, if an echo occurs too far after the original sound, it makes the noise garbled and unclear. Acoustical engineers study ways to create the right kind of echoes at the right times. Large auditoriums or concert halls frequently have high ceilings with reflective materials, either the ceilings themselves are reflective or reflective materials added to the ceilings, to bounce the sounds back to the audience. Acoustical engineers must walk a fine line between increasing the reverberation and keeping the clarity of the sound when designing such spaces.

THE DOPPLER EFFECT

The pitch of a blaring siren on a stationary ambulance would seem consistent to observers; however, if the ambulance was moving, the pitch would seem higher to the observers as the ambulance approaches them and then lower as it moves further away from them. This change in pitch is due to the **Doppler effect**, or Doppler shift.

The Doppler effect is not a special property of emergency vehicles only; it happens when any sound source is in motion relative to the observer. When a source of sound is stationary, it emits sound waves in all directions in what can be pictured as a spherical wave front. When the object begins to move, it emits sounds at the same rate as before; however, because it is moving toward sound that was previously emitted, those sound waves become closer together. The result is that the waves have a higher frequency and, thus, a higher pitch. Behind the moving object, the

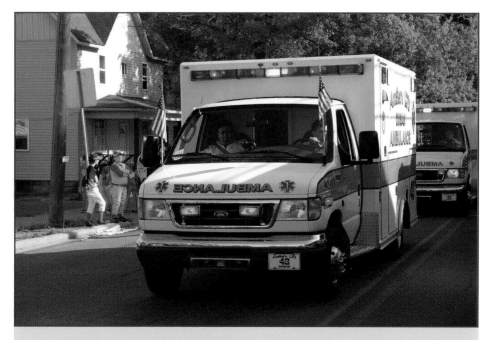

The Doppler effect causes the rise and fall in pitch of an ambulance's siren as it drives past an observer. (Courtesy of Wikimedia)

sound waves are more spaced out creating a lower frequency and lower-pitched sound wave.

The amount of change in pitch caused by the Doppler effect depends on the **relative velocity** between the source and the observer. The faster the source appears to be moving to the observer, the greater the change in pitch. For this reason, observers will not notice the Doppler effect in the everyday conversation of people as they walk by the observers because they are not moving fast enough. Since this is an effect of relative velocity between the source and the observer, the source can be stationary while the observer is moving. If a person drove by a stationary ambulance with its siren blaring, that person would hear the same change in pitch because of the Doppler effect.

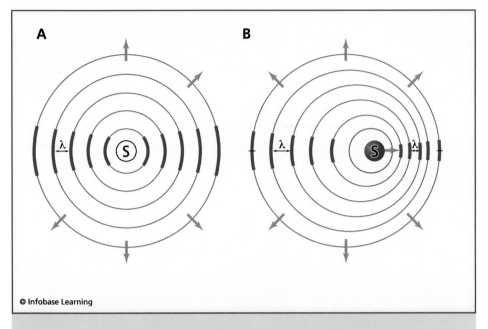

In part (A), the source (S) of sound is stationary, and the sound waves are emitted uniformly in a circular fashion. In part (B), the source is moving to the right. To a stationary observer, the sound waves propagating in that direction will be higher in frequency and shorter in wavelength. The sound waves propagating behind the moving source will be lower in frequency and longer in wavelength.

The Doppler effect is not limited to sound waves; it affects all types of waves. In terms of visible light waves, the Doppler effect creates what is known as *red shift* and *blue shift*. Astronomers want to know if an object in motion in space is moving toward Earth, or away. If objects are moving toward Earth, the Doppler effect causes the wavelengths of any light emitted to appear shortened. In the visible light spectrum, blue light has a short wavelength and is high energy; therefore, any electromagnetic wave that has a shorter wavelength as a result of the Doppler effect is called *blue shifted*, whether or not the light is actually blue or even visible. If the object is moving away from the Earth, the wavelength appears

Seeing Inside with Ultrasound

The leap from using sound to detect obstacles in water to detecting abnormalities in a person's body took some time to become accepted. By the 1920s, ultrasound was being used in medicine to treat ailments but not to diagnose them; however, the equipment used to produce ultrasounds existed in the form of metal flaw detectors. These detectors used ultrasonic waves that were passed through a piece of metal to detect places in which the metal was thin or had microscopic cracks. In 1942, Karl Theo Dussik (1908–68), a neurologist from Austria, published his paper, "On the Possibility of using Ultrasound as a Diagnostic Aid." This was the first paper published on the technique of using ultrasound for diagnostic purposes instead of therapeutic uses. He attempted to locate brain tumors by sending ultrasonic waves straight through the brain and recording them on the other side. Although scientists discovered that the thickness of the skull made this method impractical for finding brain tumors, it was the first proof that ultrasound could be used to produce images of the inside of the human body. In the late 1940s, English surgeon John Wild (1914–2009) began researching the idea of using ultrasound to measure the thickness of the bowel wall and to locate and describe obstructions in the abdomen. His research showed that malignant tumors could be diagnosed with ultrasound by their difference in density. Wild collaborated with another scientist to attempt to use ultrasound as a means to detect brain tumors, but they were unsuccessful.

In the 1950s, Scottish physician Professor Ian Donald (1910–87) largely advanced the use of ultrasounds, particularly in the areas of gynecology and obstetrics. He first used a metal flaw detector to note the ultrasonic characteristics of several tumors and cysts that he had recently removed from some of his patients. Donald worked together with an instrument technician to apply this to live patients in order to detect tumors, cysts, and other abnormalities in women's bodies. The method soon gained

(continues)

(continued)

recognition as it was noninvasive, harmless, and helped diagnose conditions that could often be corrected. In 1959, Donald noticed that clear echoes from the fetal head allowed him to make accurate measurements. As a result, this method became generally accepted for tracking the size and growth of a fetus.

The technology improved drastically over the next years with significantly clearer images and smaller, more portable equipment. In 1965, the development of the first real-time sonography equipment allowed images of a moving fetus, or beating heart, to be shown and significantly increased the functionality of ultrasounds as diagnostic tools. At the end of this decade, ultrasound imaging had been combined with Doppler imaging to produce live images that can show the velocity and direction of blood flow. The field of sonography developed extremely fast once people understood the noninvasive benefits of viewing the inside of the human body without surgery.

longer. Red light has the longest wavelength and lowest energy color of the visible spectrum; changes in this direction are called *red shifts*.

USING SOUND

Sound is used in many ways from communication and entertainment to its use as a warning of danger. All of these uses involve the production of sound within the range of human hearing. Sounds produced out of this range are also used in many different applications. Sounds produced below the range of human hearing are called **infrasound**. These extremely low-energy sounds do not have many uses because obstacles can easily absorb or block them. However, sounds produced above the range of human hearing, called **ultrasound**, are used in many different ways.

Sonar is an American term used to mean sound, navigation, and ranging, but sonar was in use before it acquired this name. Sonar encompasses the process of sending out a high-frequency sound and then measuring how long it takes for the sound to return from a reflecting object; sonar measurements are generally made underwater. The elapsed time and the speed of sound in water can be used to calculate how far away the reflecting object is located. At the beginning of the 20th century, sonar was first developed as a way to locate icebergs and prevent disasters, such as the sinking of the RMS *Titanic*. The technology was developed further during World War I as a means to detect the location of submarines. For a brief period, it was even used aboveground to discover planes in the air before the advent of radar. Currently, sonar is frequently used on boats as depth finders to find the least dangerous path for a boat to travel and as fish finders to locate the depth of fish nearby.

There are two types of sonar devices—active sonar and passive sonar. Active sonar produces its own sound and measures the time it takes for the echo of that sound to return. The method proves very useful when trying to precisely pinpoint an object; however, the disadvantages are that it does not provide information about the reflecting object and that operations involving stealth are difficult while sounds are being emitted at regular intervals. Passive sonar is much more useful in most military applications because it is silent. Passive sonar merely detects and analyzes nearby sounds to determine an exact frequency for the sounds. All ship engines make sounds; different types of engines produce sounds of a different pitch. In the past, sailors used training and databases to determine what type of ship made a specific frequency sound; however, in recent years, computers are replacing these sailors. Although passive sonar cannot easily determine an exact location, the technology can describe the reflecting object's trajectory. Measuring how the location of the sound's source changes over

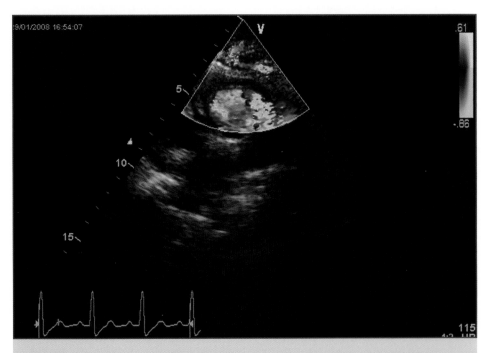

9/01/2008 16:54:07

V

.61

5

-.86

10

15

115

Echocardiograms use sound waves to create a two-dimensional image of a heart. Doppler ultrasounds add color to show the velocity of the blood flowing through the heart. (Courtesy of European Journal of Echocardiography)

time allows for the detection of the object's speed and general location.

Sound is frequently used for medical purposes to diagnose an ailment and occasionally to treat one. Ultrasonic waves used to treat an illness have a much higher energy and generally a difference in frequency or intensity or both. Ultrasonic waves can be used to bring heat (through the absorption of vibrations) into the body to treat cysts or tumors. Ultrasound can break apart kidney stones by focusing several sound waves at their location and by sending sound pulses into the patient's body. Although the process does not inflict permanent damage, it does cause some pain and discomfort for the patient, particularly if the stone is located near a bone that may vibrate when the sound pulses strike the stone.

Using ultrasonic waves to produce an image of a person's organs is typically called *medical sonography.* In sonography, a medical professional applies a probe to a patient's skin that sends out an ultrasonic wave. As the wave reflects off various surfaces and returns back to the probe, the machine translates the elapsed time and strength of the reflected wave into an image. In Doppler sonography, the change in the frequency of the returning wave is measured in order to find the velocity of a moving object, such as blood. Doppler sonography is particularly useful when examining a heart in an echocardiogram because it allows doctors to see where the blood is flowing, as well as its speed and direction. Paramedics are now using ultrasound technology in the Focused Assessment with Sonography for Trauma (FAST) exam, instead of a computerized tomography scan, to allow them to assess an individual for internal bleeding. Obstetrical ultrasound is used to assess the growth and development of a fetus in the mother's womb. Medical diagnostics have become much less invasive, dangerous, and painful since the development of sonography.

Ultrasonic waves are used in other applications as well, such as jewelry cleaning. One common way to clean jewelry is to place it in a sonicator along with water and a cleaning solution. High-frequency sound waves that are sent into the liquid cause cavitation—the formation of vapor bubbles. These bubbles act with the cleaning solution to gently scrub dirt and oils from the surface of the jewelry without causing damage. Another use of ultrasound is in the autofocus drive in some camera lenses. Friction produced by ultrasonic vibrations created within the lens is used to rotate a metallic ring that allows the camera to focus quickly and easily.

Humans are not the only creatures that use sound in their daily lives. Some animals, like bats, dolphins, and whales, use sound to help them navigate. Very much like a natural sonar, these animals produce a sound and use the reflected sound wave from an object to determine their course. Through the reflected sound wave, they detect not only the distance between them and the object but also the object's general shape and size. These animals can use their "biosonar" to hunt and locate prey. Animals that live in low-visibility areas, such as dark caves and deep in the ocean, have developed this unique ability over time. Although some of these creatures use ultrasound for their sonar, a few, such as dolphins, produce sounds within the range of human hearing.

SUMMARY

Sound starts as a vibration of the molecules within a medium. These vibrations cause the molecules to form regular patterns of compression and rarefaction, thus creating a mechanical, longitudinal wave. Sound can be produced naturally from a human or animal or artificially from speakers and musical instruments. In fact, any action that causes vibrations can create a sound. The loudness of a sound is measured in decibels, which is measured on a logarithmic scale, to show small differences easily. As decibels are always measured using a reference level, 0 dB is used as the threshold of human hearing.

Sound can be influenced and controlled through acoustics and soundproofing. Materials that do not easily transmit sound should be used to soundproof an area. These materials may either reflect the sound or absorb and change the sound. Materials that absorb sound change the energy into heat through the friction that is produced between the moving air molecules and the particles of the material. Acoustical engineers understand the need for echoes to create good acoustics for a performance area. Echoes continually move sound toward the back of the space while adding fullness to the sound; however, too many echoes can cause the sound to become distorted and unclear.

The Doppler effect occurs when there is relative motion between the source of a sound and a person listening to the sound. This effect causes the pitch and frequency of a sound wave to become higher as the source approaches the listener and then to become lower as the source moves away from the listener. People can hear this effect, for example, as an ambulance passes by them or as cars fly past at a racetrack—the engine sound starts high as the drivers approach and then slides lower as they pass. The Doppler effect is not limited to sound; it influences all types of waves, including light.

Our modern world uses sound in many different ways. One well-known use is sonar—a technology that uses sound to navigate and locate nearby objects in water. People use sonar while boating for pleasure to help them find safe and deep paths to follow and to help them locate fish in the vicinity. Sonar also has military applications in locating submarines and ships in nearby waters. Military applications of sonar are usually passive—it "listens" for sounds—instead of active—it sends out a sound periodically and waits for the echo to return to determine an object's location. Ultrasound technology has made the medical uses of sound widespread and well known. Sonography is used to safely see inside of a person's body to detect tumors or problems with various organs. When combined with Doppler imaging, the rate and direction of moving fluids, such as blood, can be determined.

The interactions of sound with the matter around it changes how sound is used in everyday life. Sound can be reflected, absorbed, or transmitted by materials, and each effect is beneficial in some situations. Sound must be reflected in an auditorium, absorbed by the walls in a recording studio, and transmitted by a person's body tissues during an ultrasound. The purpose of the sound influences what types of materials are used and what types of interactions are desired.

3

The Electromagnetic Spectrum

Chapter 3 explores the electromagnetic spectrum, beginning with an explanation of some properties of light. The rest of the chapter is devoted to a description of each part of the electromagnetic spectrum, with the exception of visible light, including its uses and natural sources. Chapter 4 will provide individual attention to visible light.

LIGHT OVERVIEW

Although the term *light* specifically refers to electromagnetic waves that are visible to the human eye, in physics the term is often used to refer to any wave on the electromagnetic spectrum, whether that wave is visible or not. For example, a person discussing the speed of light is actually referring to the speed of all electromagnetic waves. Radiation is any energy that travels and spreads out as it moves and is frequently used in place of the word *light*. The electromagnetic spectrum consists of all of the electromagnetic waves placed in order according to wavelength and frequency. The spectrum is divided into sections to show waves that are used for similar purposes and that have similar effects on

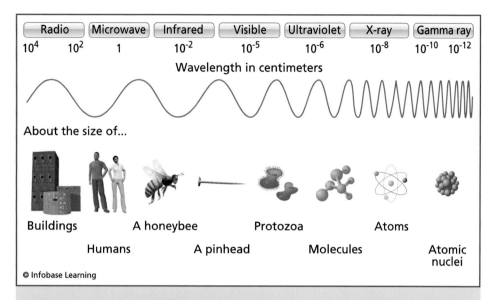

| Radio | Microwave | Infrared | Visible | Ultraviolet | X-ray | Gamma ray |

10^4 10^2 1 10^{-2} 10^{-5} 10^{-6} 10^{-8} 10^{-10} 10^{-12}

Wavelength in centimeters

About the size of...

Buildings   A honeybee   Protozoa   Atoms

Humans   A pinhead   Molecules   Atomic
nuclei

© Infobase Learning

The electromagnetic spectrum is comprised of waves of many different wavelengths. This image compares the wavelength of each type of wave to the length of common objects to give the reader a perspective on the range of sizes.

their surroundings. The spectrum is comprised of radio waves, microwaves, infrared light, visible light, ultraviolet (UV) light, X-rays, and gamma rays, and it organizes these waves in order from those with the longest wavelength and lowest frequency to those with the shortest wavelength and highest frequency, as shown in the above figure.

The wavelength and frequency of a wave affect the energy of the wave and, thus, its use and the amount of damage that it can do to the human body. Due to the fact that the spectrum divides types of waves accordingly to show similar uses and properties, the wavelength and frequency range overlaps somewhat. The following table shows the approximate ranges of wavelengths and frequencies and the change in the overall energy level of the waves throughout the spectrum.

The Electromagnetic Spectrum

TYPE OF WAVE	APPROXIMATE WAVELENGTH RANGE (m)	APPROXIMATE FREQUENCY RANGE (Hz)	ENERGY LEVEL
Radio waves	$> 1 \times 10^{-1}$	$< 1 \times 10^{9}$	Lowest energy
Microwaves	1×10^{-3}–1×10^{-1}	1×10^{8}–3×10^{11}	
Infrared light	7×10^{-7}–1×10^{-2}	1×10^{11}–4×10^{14}	
Visible light	4×10^{-7}–7×10^{-7}	4×10^{14}–8×10^{14}	
UV light	1×10^{-8}–4×10^{-7}	8×10^{14}–5×10^{16}	
X-rays	1×10^{-12}–1×10^{-7}	1×10^{16}–1×10^{21}	
Gamma rays	$< 1 \times 10^{-11}$	$> 1 \times 10^{20}$	Highest energy

Electromagnetic waves are produced through the relationship between electricity and magnetism that states that a current creates a magnetic field and that a changing magnetic field produces a current. To create an electromagnetic wave, the electric field around a charged object, such as an electron, is changed, causing a magnetic field to form. Oscillations of the electric field cause the magnetic field to change, creating a set of self-propagating conditions that strengthens the electric field and, thus, the magnetic field. The fields are formed perpendicularly to each other and create two transverse-shaped waves, as shown in the next figure.

RADIO WAVES

Radio waves have the longest wavelengths in the electromagnetic spectrum and the least amount of energy. Due to their low en-

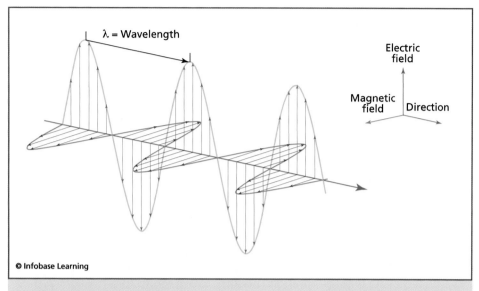

Electric and magnetic fields traveling perpendicular to one another combine to form an electromagnetic wave.

ergy, radio waves are referred to as **nonionizing radiation**, which means that the waves do not remove electrons from atoms while passing through a medium. This removal of electrons, or ionizing, can kill cells or damage deoxyribonucleic acid (DNA) molecules within cells. Although DNA can normally repair itself, when the damage is extensive or repeated several times, the radiation can cause mutations that may lead to cancer. While radio waves can pass through most things (e.g., from walls to human bodies), they are not absorbed by the medium and should not cause damage as they pass through the medium because of their low energy. Some people believe that despite the fact that radio waves are nonionizing, long-term exposure to these waves may cause cell mutation. For example, some people believe that living near radio-wave-emitting power lines can cause cancer or that using cell phones can cause brain tumors; however, the research thus far has been unable to prove a link between radio waves and

The Dual Nature of Light

Until the early part of the 19th century, scientists debated about the nature of light. Sir Isaac Newton (1643–1727), the English scientist who influenced so much of physics, theorized that light was a stream of particles. He gave the shadows produced by objects and the **reflection** of light in a straight line as evidence for his theory. The Dutch physicist Christiaan Huygens (1629–95), however, suggested that light had a wave nature because of how it bent as it moved from one medium to another. In the early 19th century, the British physicist Thomas Young (1773–1829) devised an experiment that proved that light was a wave. In his double-slit experiment, Young directed a light through two narrow slits onto a screen that he had positioned to capture how the light was affected by its passage through the slits. Young found that the light produced a regular pattern of light and dark bands on the screen. His finding could only be explained if light behaved as a wave.

These light and dark bands occurred because the waves bent outward as they passed through the small openings. As these bent waves interacted with one another, they produced larger and smaller waves. Two waves that lined up crest to crest and trough to trough strengthened one another and created a bright band on the screen. If two waves matched a crest to a trough, the two canceled one another out to produce a dark band on the screen. Chapter 7 discusses these types of wave interactions in more detail.

While Young's experiment was convincing, some still had doubts until Scottish scientist James Clark Maxwell (1831–79) devised his math-

cancer. A study on the relationship between cell phone usage and brain tumors called the *Interphone Study*, which was published online in 2010, concludes, "Overall, no increase in risk of glioma or meningioma [two common types of brain tumors] was observed with use of mobile phones."

ematical theory of electromagnetism. This theory led to proof that light consisted of an electric field and a magnetic field moving together in waveform. These equations even mathematically solved for the same speed of light that had been experimentally found nearly 200 years previously. Thus, the wave theory of light reigned supreme until the 20th century.

In 1905, Albert Einstein (1879–1955), the famous German physicist, concluded that light could be considered a particle, or **photon**, through several complex calculations. His idea provided a reason for the **photoelectric effect**, whereby metal emits electrons when it is struck by light. Einstein pictured light traveling as a stream of photons with each photon containing a set amount of energy. American physicist Arthur Compton (1892–1962) further added to the particle theory of light by using it to explain why some parts of X-rays were scattered to the sides of the original beam with a longer wavelength than they had before scattering. He explained this scattering as a collision between photons and electrons, whereby the longer wavelengths resulted from the conservation of energy of the system.

Research has proven that light has both wave and particle properties, and, thus, light has a "dual nature"—that is, it is both a particle and a wave. Within a few more years, this theory had been expanded to state that all matter has wave and particle natures, even macroscopic items like people. The reason the wave nature is not detectable with large-scale items is that the wavelength is extremely small.

Communication is the primary use of radio waves in modern technology. Radio waves carry signals to radios that are converted into sound and music. The longest-wavelength radio waves are used to transmit AM radio stations, whereas shorter-wavelength waves are used to transmit FM stations. The shortest-wavelength radio waves are used for police radios, military radios, and other types of person-to-person communication. Radio waves are also used to transmit television signals before these signals are sent through cables and into homes. Cell phones use radio waves to send signals to and from cell phone towers.

Some natural sources of radio waves include the Sun and other astronomical objects. Radio telescopes can be used to detect these waves and to transmit information to computers. Radio waves have aided scientists in locating several galaxies that they may not have otherwise been able to detect. Lightning strikes can also produce radio waves, which is why a thunderstorm may degrade the clarity of a radio signal.

MICROWAVES

Microwaves are just above radio waves in terms of energy with slightly shorter wavelengths and higher frequency. Microwaves are also nonionizing radiation, yet they are slightly more dangerous to the human body in other ways. Microwaves are absorbed by water molecules that become hot very quickly and can cause damaging burns. Although microwaves would not cause cancer, prolonged exposure to intense amounts of microwaves would cause serious thermal damage to a person. The lens of the eye is particularly sensitive to thermal damage, and large amounts of microwave exposure have been shown to cause cataracts. Microwaves, however, are easily stopped by metal, which is why microwave ovens are safe. The metal walls and metal screen within the glass door of microwave ovens prevent most of the waves from escaping. The amount of exposure needed to damage the human body is significantly more than the small amount of microwaves that can leak from a microwave oven.

Microwaves have other uses besides heating food in a microwave oven. They are used for some types of communication and are primarily used to transmit long-distance phone calls to communication satellites. Most types of radar used microwaves, including Doppler weather radar. Radar uses the echo of reflected microwaves to detect the location of objects, and Doppler radar uses the Doppler effect to determine the speed of moving objects, such as rain clouds. The Global Positioning System (GPS) uses microwaves to communicate navigational information between a receiver and satellites. The medical community has recently used microwaves to kill tumors in patients in a process called *microwave ablation*. In this process, a microwave antenna is placed directly into a tumor, and microwaves are sent to the antenna. The antenna sends microwaves into the tumor cells whose water molecules absorb the heat and cause cell death.

The natural sources of microwave radiation are minimal and largely astronomical. In 1964, American physicists Arno Penzias (1933–) and Robert Wilson (1936–) accidentally discovered background noise caused by microwaves emanating from every direction at once. This background noise has since been called *cosmic microwave background radiation* and is frequently listed as proof for the **big bang theory**.

INFRARED LIGHT

Infrared light falls between microwaves and visible light on the electromagnetic spectrum. Infrared is typically broken into two parts: (1) the waves closest to visible light on the spectrum are called *near infrared* and (2) the waves furthest from visible light are called *far infrared*. Far infrared waves are felt as heat, whereas the near infrared waves cannot be seen or felt. All infrared light is nonionizing radiation; however, far infrared light can cause burns and related heat damage.

Far infrared lights are used to provide heat in many different ways. Fast food restaurants use heat lamps to keep food warm until it is served. These waves have also recently been used as thermal therapy for injuries, particularly in sports. All living creatures release infrared light in the form of heat, thus, night-vision goggles can be used to detect infrared light and produce an image with visible light. Infrared imaging can be used to detect and locate a person in a collapsed building or to find components of a machine that are overheating and may fail. Near infrared light is used in remote controls to send a signal to a television

Heat lamps use infrared light rays to keep food warm. (Courtesy of RoadFood.com)

across a room. Some snakes have sensory pits on their heads that detect infrared light and help it locate prey in a lightless area, such as a cave.

Objects cool down by releasing energy in the form of infrared light. Any object above absolute zero has the potential to emit some degree of infrared radiation, whether it is heat that it produces itself, such as in a living creature, or heat that it absorbs from other sources, like water in a pool cooling after being warmed by the Sun. Most objects also reflect some infrared light—some better than others. Covering a building with infrared reflective materials would help keep the inside of the building cooler as these materials reflect heat from the Sun instead of absorbing it.

ULTRAVIOLET LIGHT

UV light has wavelengths just shorter than those of visible light waves. Low-energy UV waves that are closest to visible light on the spectrum are nonionizing radiation. Higher-energy UV waves are classified as **ionizing radiation**. The electromagnetic spectrum does not have a specific area in which light becomes ionizing radiation because the amount of energy needed to remove electrons depends on the specific atoms from which the electrons are being removed.

All types of UV waves damage collagen fibers in a person's skin, causing wrinkles and premature aging. Even limited exposure to UV light can cause sunburn, which is a body's reaction to DNA damage caused by ionizing radiation. The body attempts to repair the damage in several ways, including prompting skin to produce more melanin that helps prevent future damage by harmlessly turning UV photons into heat. Repeated or extreme exposure to UV light can damage eyes or cause various types of skin cancer when the damage to DNA becomes too significant. Thankfully, the atmosphere absorbs the majority of the UV radiation emitted by the Sun, and a person can be protected from the remaining rays in a number of ways, including the use of sunscreen and UV-absorbing glass in windows.

Despite the possibility of danger, UV waves have many applications in the modern world. UV lamps, or "black lights," emit both UV light and violet light from the visible spectrum. Most white clothes will fluoresce, or appear to glow, when they are under black light because whitening agents are added to most laundry detergents. These whitening agents absorb UV light and convert it into blue or violet visible light. The addition of this blue or violet light counteracts the natural yellowing of white clothes that occurs as they age and makes them seem a brighter white. UV lamps can also be used to detect traces of bodily fluids, such as blood, at a crime scene even if such traces are not visible under normal lighting. Inks and fibers that reflect UV light are frequently used for security purposes, such as in passports and in dollar bills, to help prevent forgery. UV light can also be used to kill bacteria and sterilize medical equipment, air, and even water.

Any extremely hot astronomical object, including the Sun, emits UV light. The majority of this light is filtered by Earth's atmosphere, although UV telescopes have been placed on satellites

X-ray for the Perfect Fit

As X-ray machines became popular for medical purposes but before the dangers of radiation were understood, X-rays were used for more mundane purposes, such as the perfect fit for a customer at a shoe store. A customer would step onto a ledge on the machine and slip his or her feet into an opening under which an X-ray tube was positioned. The customer and the shoe salesman would then view the X-rayed image of the customer's feet through portals to check that the shoes fit properly and did not cause any pinching. These machines were popular in the 1920s, 1930s, and 1940s as they were hyped as the best way to ensure proper fitting shoes, particularly for children. The customers' exposure to X-rays from these machines was not extreme, but the shoe salesmen who operated them were frequently exposed to more radiation than was generally healthy; some injuries were reported. By the 1950s, the dangers of radiation exposure were better understood, and the machines fell into disuse.

This shoe fluoroscope, manufactured by Adrain Shoe Fitter, Inc., was used in a Washington, D.C., shoe store in 1938. (Courtesy of the National Museum of Health and Medicine)

in space to monitor the emission of UV radiation. UV light is also unintentionally produced when electric arcs are used for industrial uses, such as arc welding.

X-RAYS

X-rays are the next highest-energy electromagnetic wave on the spectrum, and because of their very small wavelength and high frequency, they often behave more like photons than waves. German physicist Wilhelm Röntgen (1895–1923) accidentally discovered X-rays and used the "X" in the name to indicate that these rays were an unknown quantity. The name has persisted despite further discovery and an understanding of the nature of X-rays. X-rays are ionizing radiation, and prolonged or repeated exposure can cause mutations in DNA and can cause cancer. For this reason, radiologists stand behind a screen while giving X-rays, and patients wear lead to prevent exposure to other parts of their bodies.

The most common use of X-rays is for the medical imaging of bones and organs within a person. As X-rays are sent through a person's body, they pass completely through skin, muscle, and tissue and are absorbed by bones and other dense objects. The X-rays that pass through skin, muscle, and tissue are captured on X-ray film on the other side of the person and produce clear images of their bones. X-rays are similarly used in airport security to detect dense materials, like metal and hard plastic, in bags. X-ray crystallography is used by chemists to discover the relative position of atoms within the compounds that they produce, which helps in the development of possible applications of the compound. X-rays can be used for the nondestructive testing of welds to detect unevenness in the density of the weld that may cause weakness and future leakage.

There are many cosmic sources for X-rays, such as the Sun, black holes, stars, and some comets. None of the X-rays from these sources penetrate the atmosphere to reach Earth's surface; therefore, X-ray telescopes are typically placed on satellites. Detecting X-rays from cosmic sources provides scientists with additional information about celestial objects, which they may not have otherwise found.

GAMMA RAYS

Gamma rays are the highest-energy waves on the electromagnetic spectrum with the smallest wavelengths and highest frequencies. These rays are the most penetrating ionizing radiation, and, thus, they cause the most damage in terms of cell death, DNA mutation, and cancer. The penetration of this radiation can also cause more widespread damage, such as radiation sickness. Gamma rays can cause damage either through external exposure, whereby a radioactive source emits rays that enter the body from outside, or through internal exposure, whereby a radioactive source is ingested or inhaled and emits the rays within the body.

The deadly nature of gamma rays is used in a process called *irradiation* to kill bacteria and to prevent the spoilage of food. Unlike canning and freezing processes, irradiation helps food last longer without losing nutrients. Irradiation passes gamma rays through food to kill bacteria without causing the food to be dangerous to future consumers. Gamma-knife surgery is used to kill cancer cells by directing several gamma rays at a cancerous tumor from different angles so that only the intended area receives the maximum dosage of radiation. Radioactive tracers are substances with slight radioactivity that patients ingest to allow doctors to view their bodily processes. For example, after a patient swallows a radioactive tracer, the gamma rays that the substance emits are recorded to see how the patient's intestines are functioning.

Gamma rays are produced by high-energy events in the universe, such as supernova explosions and black holes. Luckily, these rays never penetrate Earth's atmosphere and are unable to cause damage. Nuclear reactions produce gamma rays to release energy when bonds are broken or formed. Radioactive materials typically release gamma rays as they decay into more stable atoms. One particularly deadly example is radon-222, a radioactive gas that is produced by the normal decay of uranium found in soil and rocks. Radon gas can build up in places, particularly in basements, that are enclosed and surrounded by soil. Once radon gas is inhaled and has entered a person's bloodstream, it can decay and release gamma rays and other radioactive particles and cause cancer.

SUMMARY

In physics, light, electromagnetic radiation, and electromagnetic waves are all words for the same thing—energy that travels as a wave and does not require a medium through which to travel. The electromagnetic spectrum organizes all of these types of waves in order from those with the longest wavelength to those with the shortest wavelength. As the wavelength of a wave decreases, the frequency and energy level both increase along this spectrum. In order from the longest to shortest wavelength, the electromagnetic spectrum consists of radio waves, microwaves, infrared light, visible light, UV light, X-rays, and gamma rays. Light waves are transverse waves that travel through the vibration of electric and magnetic fields that are perpendicular to one another.

Electromagnetic waves can be broken into two categories: ionizing radiation and nonionizing radiation. Ionizing radiation (e.g., higher-energy UV light, X-rays, and gamma rays) has enough energy to remove electrons and damage cells and DNA as it travels through an object. Nonionizing radiation (e.g., radio waves, microwaves, infrared light, visible light, and some wavelengths of UV light) has less energy, but this type of radiation is not completely harmless. Prolonged or extreme amounts of exposure can produce injury. Microwaves can cause burns, infrared light can lead to heat stroke, and even nonionizing UV light can damage skin and cause wrinkles. These types of waves are useful for many things because they can travel long distances through both air and space. Radio waves are primarily used for communication from cell phones to television signals. Microwaves are used to help prepare dinner more quickly and to predict weather with Doppler weather radar. Infrared light is used to keep food hot and to help the military see in the dark. UV lamps like "black lights" are used for entertainment, forensics, and security purposes. The relative safety of nonionizing radiation makes it extremely useful in our modern world.

Although the three types of ionizing radiation—higher-energy UV light, X-rays, and gamma rays—are useful, they must be applied under controlled circumstances and with as little exposure

as possible. Higher-energy UV light can be used for the steriliza-
tion of objects and even air. X-rays are used to image the bones
in a person's body to locate breaks and malformations. Gamma
rays are used to kill bacteria in irradiation to prolong the shelf life
of fresh food and to target and destroy cancer cells. Despite the
dangers, these rays have aided in several medical advancements
that have helped improve the quality of life for many people. Because light has so many different uses today, one should understand what light is and be aware of the type of light that is applied
in each situation, whether for medical use or for simply heating
last night's leftovers. Understanding the different types of light
and the dangers that each of these electromagnetic waves presents
is vital to understanding the way that light interacts with matter.

4

Color

Although the visible portion of electromagnetic spectrum is only a tiny portion of the entire spectrum, it is responsible for *all* the color that we see in our world. Chapter 4 focuses on the colors that make up visible light and on their interaction with one another. The production of color differs, depending on whether the color is produced by lights, such as within a television screen, or whether the color is produced by dyes, such as the designs on a t-shirt. Chapter 4 also explains color perception—that is, why a rose is perceived as red and why the sky is perceived as blue.

THE RAINBOW

The visible light portion of the electromagnetic spectrum contains a range of colors familiar to most people as those of the rainbow. In order from the longest to the shortest wavelength, these colors are red, orange, yellow, green, blue, indigo, and violet. People frequently use the mnemonic, ROY G. BIV, to help them remember the colors and their order. Infrared light is just below the color red in the electromagnetic spectrum, and ultraviolet (UV) light is just above violet. Red light is the lowest-energy visible light,

Rainbows occur when visible light is dispersed through raindrops into all seven colors. Double rainbows like this one occur when light is reflected twice before being dispersed. (Courtesy of a Pennsylvania State University climatologist)

whereas violet light has the most energy. **White light** is produced when all the colors of the visible spectrum are together in equal amounts. The Sun is the best producer of true white light because most artificial lighting contains all the colors but in an uneven distribution. The light from incandescent light bulbs produces a "warm" feeling because these bulbs tend to have an abundance of light from the red end of the spectrum. Fluorescent lights can produce either a bluer, "cool" light or a light similar to incandescent bulbs, depending on the coating applied to the inside of the bulb.

When any light is passed through a prism, it undergoes **dispersion**— that is, it breaks out into all the colors of light that it contains. A rainbow is created if the original light contains all of the visible colors. If this dispersed light were passed through a second prism, all the colors could recombine to form white light. The colors are separated because of their different wavelengths and frequencies, which is why the colors are always seen in the same order even if some colors are faint or missing altogether. Rainbows occur in the sky when droplets of water within the air act as tiny prisms to disperse sunlight as it passes through. This separation of colors is due to a property called **refraction**, which chapter 5 will discuss in greater depth.

Some objects in the world are called **luminous** because they produce their own light, like the Sun. Nonluminous objects do not produce any light; however, they may reflect the light emitted by luminous objects, for example, the Moon reflecting light from the Sun. Luminous objects can be classified according to how they produce their light. Incandescent light sources produce light caused by heat. For example, incandescent light bulbs contain a thin filament of wire that becomes hot as electricity is passed through it; as the filament grows hot, it begins to glow and give off light. Some sources produce light through electrical discharge. This event occurs when electricity passing through a gas causes the electrons to absorb energy and jump to higher energy levels. The electrons release this absorbed energy as light, such as in neon lights, as they fall back to their original positions. Fluorescent light sources produce visible light while they are exposed to other types of electromagnetic radiation. Fluorescent light bulbs produce UV light through the excitement of gases within the tube. This UV light is absorbed by a coating applied to the side of the tube and released as visible light. Phosphorescent light sources produce light after being exposed to another light source, such as glow in the dark stickers and inks.

WHAT MAKES A ROSE RED?

Nonluminous objects must depend on reflecting light to appear a certain color. When the same sunlight strikes a rose, however, the petals of the rose appear red, and the leaves appear green.

The rose petals absorb all of the visible colors *except* red and reflect only the red light back to an observer's eye. The leaves absorb every color of the spectrum except green and reflect only the green light back to the observer's eye. An object appears white when all the colors of light are reflected by the object; an object appears black when all the colors of light are absorbed by the object. This absorption of color is why black and other dark-colored cars become hot so quickly; the dark paint absorbs all, or almost all, of the sunlight that strikes the surface.

Considering that the Sun is our best source of white light, it may seem surprising that it appears yellow, not white, when viewed from Earth. When viewed from outside our atmosphere, the Sun does, in fact, appear to be white. As sunlight passes through our atmosphere, the longer red wavelengths pass straight through, whereas the shorter blue wavelengths get absorbed by particles in the atmosphere and are scattered in all directions. An observer sees this scattered blue light in every direction; therefore, the sky appears to be blue. When an observer looks straight up at the Sun, however, he or she sees the colors of light that have traveled straight through the atmosphere without scattering. When the blue end of the spectrum is removed from white light, the resulting light takes on a yellowish hue. The Sun appears to turn first orange and then red as it begins to set because as it moves toward the horizon, the light that it emits must travel through more atmosphere in order to reach an observer's eye. The more atmosphere through which the light must travel, the more scattered the shorter wavelengths of light become; this process eventually leaves just the longest red wavelengths.

There is one final interesting question about the color of objects—why is the ocean blue? This question has more than one answer. One reason that the ocean water is blue is because it is reflecting the blue color of the sky. Thus, the ocean looks darker on stormy days when the sky is darker. Another reason is that the water of the ocean naturally absorbs the longer wavelengths of light, thus leaving only blue colors to be reflected. Additionally,

Rose petals are red because they reflect red light, whereas the leaves are green because they reflect green light. (Courtesy of Kriyayoga.com)

ocean water frequently contains particulates that absorb more of specific colors and less of others. Thus, some beaches have water that is greener or bluer than others.

ADDITIVE COLORS

Additive color mixing is the process of adding colored lights together to create new colors. This process is the opposite of most types of color production undertaken today (e.g., dyed fabric and painted walls). In 1861, James Maxwell (1831–79), the Scottish physicist whose equations helped prove the wave nature of light, demonstrated that color photographs could be made using addi-

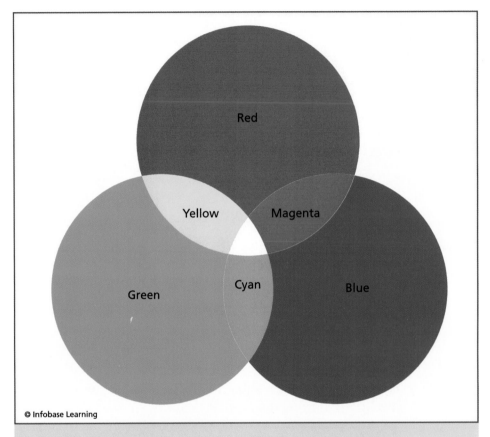

The primary additive colors—blue, green, and red—combine to form white.

tive colors. This demonstration was the first of its kind to use additive colors and to show their possible usefulness. Maxwell had three pictures taken of a tartan ribbon—the first using a red filter, the second using a green filter, and the third using a blue filter. These pictures were developed into slides and were projected using a lantern and the same colored filter that was used to take the picture. The result was one red and black image, one green and black image, and one blue and black image. Maxwell projected the three images overlapping each other and formed an image with all the colors of the original tartan ribbon. His demonstration eventually led to the first color photographic film in the early 20th century.

The additive color process begins with black and gradually lightens to white as colored lights are added. The **primary additive colors** are red, blue, and green. White light is produced if all three of these colored lights are present in even ratios. The presence of only two of the colors, as shown in the figure on page 56, produces one of the secondary additive colors—cyan, magenta, or yellow. Any color can be produced by adding primary colors in even and uneven ratios. Additive light mixing is used to produce images with colored light, such as with televisions and computer monitors.

SUBTRACTIVE COLORS

The subtractive color method produces most of the color seen in the world. In this method, specific colors within white light are absorbed, or subtracted, to produce a desired color. The color black results when all the colors in white light are absorbed. The leaves and petals of a rose produce their colors in this fashion. In the early 18th century, Jakob Le Blon (1667–1741), a German painter and engraver, developed three- and four-color printing methods based on the subtractive colors. The colors he used were red, blue, and yellow with black sometimes added as an optional fourth color. These are very close to the **primary subtractive colors**

(continues on page 60)

Subtractive Color Mixing

PRIMARY COLORS MIXED		SECONDARY COLOR PRODUCED
Magenta	Cyan	Blue
Magenta	Yellow	Red
Yellow	Cyan	Green

Television Screens

There are three main types of televisions currently in use: cathode-ray tube (CRT), plasma, and liquid crystal display (LCD) televisions. Regardless of the type of television, lighting up pixels forms images. A pixel consists of a red, blue, and green dot together. These dots light up individually or in some mixture to create specific colors through additive color mixing. The image on a television screen is made of thousands or even millions

Newer televisions, such as LCD and plasma televisions, are much smaller and less bulky than older CRT televisions. (Courtesy of Soyea)

of pixels, all of which the human brain interprets as a single image. If a person looks very closely at an image in a newspaper or one produced by his or her computer printer, he or she will probably see that each picture is really made up of very small dots. The dots seen from a distance appear as a composite image made of smooth lines. The smaller the dots, the clearer and smoother the image appears. For this reason, more pixels are better in terms of televisions, computer monitors, and digital cameras. If more pixels are used to create the image, the pixels must be smaller.

CRT televisions were the primary color televisions in most homes until recent years. In these televisions, the cathode emits a streams of electrons that moves through the tube to strike the screen at the far end. Along the way, this stream is moved by its interactions with a changing magnetic field, thus allowing it to strike specific spots along the screen at specific instants. Along the inside of the screen are three different phosphors arranged in small dots to form the pixels of the image. Three different electron beams—one red, one blue, and one green—correspond to the three different phosphors. When an electron beam strikes a phosphor, it glows its appropriate color. The electron beams "paint" the screen moving from side to side across the screen, completing a row before moving down. In a CRT television, all rows of pixels can be lit up approximately 60 times per second to form a new image. CRT televisions are falling out of favor because of the bulk packaging needed to accommodate the cathode ray tube, particularly for larger televisions.

Although many people still have CRT televisions in their homes, the vast majority of televisions sold today are plasma televisions or LCD televisions. These televisions are thinner, less bulky, and provide a clearer picture. Although plasma and LCD televisions create images through the lighting of pixels individually, the way in which the pixels themselves are formed is different. In a plasma television, there are thousands of tiny cells placed between two pieces of glass. Each cell is filled with xenon or neon gas and is lined with tiny electrodes. When these electrodes are turned on, the gas within the cell is ionized and releases UV photons. The UV photons strike a phosphor coating on the inside of the cell, causing it to glow red, green, or blue. Each pixel in a plasma television is made up of three cells—one for each of the primary colors.

In an LCD television, a layer of liquid crystals is pressed between two transparent panels that contain electrodes and polarizing filters. A polarizing filter allows light rays to pass through in one specific direction only, effectively blocking about one-half of the light from passing through. A liquid crystal is a substance that may flow like a liquid, but it forms crystal shapes like a solid. Behind this layer are fluorescent lights that produce white light. When electricity passes through the electrodes, the crystals change their orientation to allow varying amounts of light (from all the light to none) to pass through. Each pixel has three cells that contain colored filters to color the white light red, blue, or green. Some LCD display applications use light-emitting diodes to produce the white light instead of fluorescent lights. The use of these diodes allows for the production of thinner displays, such as those in many types of cell phones and portable media devices and in some televisions. However, the expense of producing large light-emitting diodes has prevented their widespread use in televisions. Although there are benefits to each type of television, all three rely on the physics of additive color mixing.

This 1877 photograph by Louis Ducos du Hauron (1837–1920), a French pioneer of color photography, was one of the first photographs to use subtractive color mixing. (Courtesy of Wikimedia)

(continued from page 57)
of cyan, magenta, and yellow, which are used in most color print-ers with or without black. The three primary colors have shifted from the red and blue because colors appear more vivid when cyan and magenta are used instead.

Subtractive color mixing is most commonly used for produc-ing dyes, pigments, and paints. Painters would find it difficult to keep every color on hand; however, they can produce any color by mixing just cyan, magenta, and yellow. Black is also frequently added as a fourth color, even though adding equal amounts of the previous three colors can produce it. The table on page 57 shows how adding just two of the primary colors will produce secondary subtractive colors.

Subtractive color mixing is based on the assumption that the light that strikes a surface will be white light and thus will contain equal amounts of all colors within the visible spectrum. When the light that strikes a surface is not truly white light, a person's eyes can generally adjust to the difference and still see the correct color with some slight variations. For this reason, clothes may appear to match underneath one light source, such as fluorescent lights in a store, and not underneath another, such as sunlight outside or incandescent lights in a home.

SUMMARY

Visible light can be considered the most important portion of the electromagnetic spectrum because it is one of the main ways that people interact with the world. Visible light consists of seven colors—red, orange, yellow, green, blue, indigo, and violet—in order from the lowest to the highest energy. Any object that emits light that it produces is called luminous, and nonluminous objects can reflect or absorb light. A luminous object can produce its light through electrical discharge, heat (incandescent), while being exposed to light (fluorescent) or after being exposed to light (phosphorescent).

When most objects appear to be a certain color, they are reflecting that color of light and absorbing all other colors. For example, an apple is red because it is reflecting red light and absorbing the rest of the colors. The color of the sky is caused by the atmospheric scattering of blue light in all directions so that blue appears to emanate from the entire sky. When the Sun begins to set, the light has to travel through more atmosphere, thus scattering more of the longer wavelength of light and eventually leaving only the red light to travel straight through.

Two color mixing methods are used to produce colors—additive and subtractive. The additive color mixing method starts with black and adds colored lights to produce a certain color. The primary additive colors are red, blue, and green. White light is produced when all three of these colors are present in even amounts. Additive color mixing is used in television and computer monitors. In subtractive color mixing, an object starts out white, reflecting all colors of light. Colors are added to absorb, or subtract, different wavelengths of light. The primary subtractive colors are cyan, magenta, and yellow, which produce black when they are added together. Subtractive color mixing is used in dyes, paints, and printers.

Reflection and Mirrors

Chapter 5 focuses on why and how reflections form, particularly in mirrors. The three types of mirrors—plane, concave, and convex—are discussed, including the types of images that each one forms depending on the position of the object. The chapter explains how to draw ray diagrams for concave and convex mirrors to show where an image will appear, whether it will be upright, and whether it will be enlarged or reduced in size compared to the object. Finally, the chapter discusses uses for all three types of mirrors.

The remaining chapters in the book will use the ray model to show how light interacts with the objects around it. The ray model does not suggest that light is a ray; instead, it allows pictures and diagrams to depict light as a ray. The rays indicate the path that the light waves and light photons are traveling. Although not entirely accurate, the rays help show how light interacts with the objects around it in the simplest way.

LAW OF REFLECTION

When light strikes a surface, some of the light is absorbed, whereas other rays are reflected and bounced back toward the observer.

The type of material that the light strikes determines how much is absorbed and how much is reflected; it also determines whether the reflection creates a clear image. The **law of reflection** helps explain why some materials create clear images and why others do not. The law of reflection states that the angle of incidence is equal to the angle of reflection for any wave striking a surface. The angle of incidence is the angle between the incoming, or incident, light ray and the **normal**—a line that is perpendicular to the surface at the point at which the light ray hits. The angle of reflection is the angle between the reflected light ray and the normal.

When light strikes a smooth surface, all the incoming light rays reflect according to the law of reflection. The light rays reflect in the same position and produce a clear image called a **specular reflection**, or regular reflection. A clear image is produced because the normal for each incidence light ray is in the same direction. When a surface is rough, reflection does not create a clear image because of **diffuse reflection**. In this case, the light rays still follow the law of reflection; however, the uneven surface causes the light rays to reflect in different directions because the normal for each incident light ray is in a different direction. A person looking into a mirror sees an unmistakable image of his or her face because of specular reflection. When the person looks at the wall on which the mirror is hung, however, the light rays bouncing off his or her face are still being reflected from the wall, but the rough surface causes a diffuse (spread out) reflection.

WHAT IS A MIRROR?

In physics, a mirror can be considered any surface that is smooth enough to create a specular reflection. As early as 3000 B.C.E., the inhabitants of Southern Mesopotamia were using metal mirrors and recording them in drawings and text. Venetian glassmakers in the 16th century first developed the precursors to today's mirrors by coating the back of a piece of glass with mercury to produce a highly reflective surface. The toxicity of mercury eventually led to the application of either molten tin or molten silver as the coating for the back of glass; an artisan would apply a series of tin or sliver coatings to protect and enhance the mirror.

PLANE MIRRORS

The first type of mirror is a **plane mirror**—a mirror with a smooth, flat surface, such as the types of mirrors found in homes. Light rays approach the mirror and bounce off it according to the law of reflection. A person's brain does not interpret the rays as bending and "sees" the light rays as coming from inside of the mirror. All light rays appear to be originating from a source inside of, or behind, the mirror in which the image is formed. This image is called a **virtual image** because the light rays do not actually meet where they appear to converge. The image formed by a plane mirror is oriented in the same vertical direction as the object that it is reflecting; therefore, the image is said to be an upright image. Because the image is the same size as the object, it is neither reduced nor magnified.

A common misconception is that a mirror reverses left and right when producing an image. This idea springs from the fact that left and right are subjective perceptions and are different depending on the situation. In fact, a mirror only reverses "in" and "out" directions or directions perpendicular to the mirror's surface. If a man standing in front of a mirror raises his right hand, the image appears to raise its left hand; however, the hand raised by the image is still on the man's right side. His perception is that the image in the mirror has raised its left hand; however, the image has no concept of left and right, and measurements of this kind must be from the man's point of view. If nonsubjective directions like north, south, east, and west are used, it is more obvious that no side-to-side reversal occurs. For example, if the man's right hand points to the east, the image's hand appears to be pointing east as well. Reversal occurs only in directions perpendicular to the mirror's surface. If the man points toward the mirror and that direction is north, then the image appears to be pointing out of the mirror toward the south.

CONCAVE MIRRORS

The second type of mirror is a **concave mirror**—a mirror that curves inward or has a "caved-in" surface, such as the inside surface of a spoon. A concave mirror is sometimes called a *converging mirror* because after the light rays bounce off the mirror, they usually come together at a point called the *focal point, F.* The focal point is always half the distance from the mirror's surface to its center of curvature, C, along a straight line called the *principal axis.* If a curved mirror extended completely to create a sphere, the center of that sphere would be the center of curvature, thus the amount of curve in a concave mirror determines how far from the mirror's surface the center of curvature and the focal point exist.

This concave mirror is producing an enlarged and upright virtual image. (Courtesy of Gayle Sutherland)

A concave mirror can create both a virtual image and **real image,** depending on where the object is placed. In a real image, the light rays truly cross at a given point, and these images can be projected onto a screen. Some images are upright, whereas others are inverted; however, in both cases, the base of the image is still on the principal axis. Images can also be either reduced in size compared to the object, or magnified. All of these possibilities depend on how close the object is to the mirror's surface. The table below provides a further explanation.

In most of the cases of a common concave mirror, such as a spoon, real images are not typically seen because the focal length is so great that objects beyond this point are too far away to produce clear images. In cases in which the concave mirror is greatly curved and the focal length is less, real images can be formed, and they look as though they are "floating" in the air in front of the mirror. The figure on page 68 shows a concave mirror producing this type of image.

Ray diagrams are frequently used to determine where an image will be located—these diagrams trace three light rays from the top of the object resting on the principal axis and show the rays reflecting off the mirror. The point at which those light rays cross again is where the top of the image will appear, and the rest of the

Types of Images Formed by Concave Mirrors

LOCATION OF OBJECT	REAL OR VIRTUAL IMAGE?	UPRIGHT OR INVERTED IMAGE?	REDUCED OR MAGNIFIED IMAGE?
Between the focal point and the mirror	Virtual	Upright	Magnified
Between the center of curvature and the focal point	Real	Inverted	Magnified
Beyond the center of curvature	Real	Inverted	Reduced

Ray Diagram for a Concave Mirror

RAY	RAY ORIENTATION	RAY MOVEMENT
1	Parallel to the principal axis	This ray starts parallel to the principal axis and passes through the focal point, *F*, after reflecting off the mirror.
2	Ray traveling through the focal point	This ray passes through the focal point, *F*, on its way to the mirror and is parallel to the principal axis after reflecting off the mirror.
3	Ray reflected on the same path	This ray passes through the center of curvature, *C*, and reflects back along the same path.

image will extend to the principal axis. Ray diagrams can also be done with only two rays; the third ray is used only to improve accuracy. The table above lists the three rays most commonly drawn to locate images formed by a concave mirror.

In some cases, not all lines on a ray diagram can be shown. For example, when the object is in front of the center of curvature in

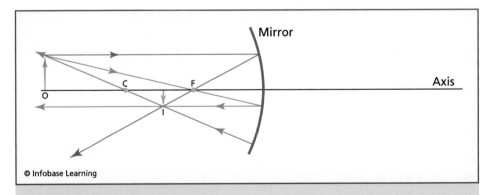

© Infobase Learning

Ray 1 (red arrow), Ray 2 (green arrow), and Ray 3 (blue arrow) intersect and form an image (I) that is real, inverted, and reduced in size.

a concave mirror, Ray 3 cannot be drawn. Because the center of curvature is behind the object, a light ray cannot leave the top of the object and travel through the center of curvature before striking the mirror without bending. When a virtual image is created, the lines will not actually meet after reflecting off the mirror; instead, the lines must be traced back through the mirror to the point at which the reflected rays appear to originate. A diagram drawn to scale can even provide the exact height of the image and its distance from the mirror.

CONVEX MIRRORS

The final type of mirror is a **convex mirror**—a mirror that curves outward toward the object that it is reflecting. Like a concave mirror, a convex mirror has a focal point, a center of curvature, and a principal axis that can help determine the location of images formed. However, the focal point and center of curvature in a convex mirror are both behind the mirror on the inside of the curve. If the mirror were to continue its curve to complete a sphere, the object would be outside of the sphere, the center of curvature would still be in the center, and the focal point would be located halfway between the center of curvature and the mirror's inside surface. A convex mirror is sometimes called a diverging mirror because the light rays spread out away from each other after they strike the mirror's surface.

A convex mirror always creates an image that is virtual, upright, and reduced in size, regardless of where the object is placed, because the focal point and center of curvature are both on the opposite side of the mirror from the object; the object's position can never change relative to these two points. This is shown in the figure on page 70. Because a convex mirror produces an image that is reduced in size but still upright, these mirrors are commonly used when an observer wants to view more area than is possible with another type of mirror. For example, convex mirrors are used for the side mirrors of cars because they show a wider view span; however, these mirrors do make objects look smaller and, thus, further away. For this reason, most side

Ray Diagram for a Convex Mirror

RAY	RAY ORIENTATION	RAY MOVEMENT
1	Parallel to the principal axis	This ray starts parallel to the principal axis and appears to originate from the focal point, *F*, after reflecting off the mirror.
2	Ray traveling through the focal point	This ray travels toward the focal point, *F*, and is parallel to the principal axis after reflecting off the mirror.
3	Ray reflected on the same path	This ray travels toward the center of curvature, *C*, and bounces back on the same path after reflecting off the mirror.

mirrors carry a warning that objects in the mirror are closer than they appear.

Ray diagrams can also be drawn for a convex mirror to predict the type of image that will be formed. The three rays used for a convex mirror are generally similar to those used for a concave mirror. Minor changes are made because the object is on the opposite side of the mirror from the focal point and center of curva-

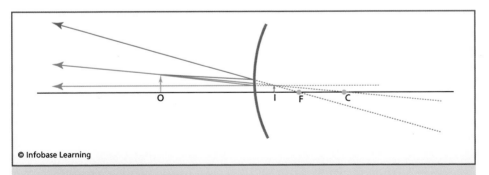

© Infobase Learning

Ray 1 (red arrow), Ray 2 (green arrow), and Ray 3 (blue arrow) intersect and form an image (I) that is virtual, upright, and reduced in size.

ture. The previous table shows the three rays drawn to locate an image formed by a convex mirror.

LOCATING AN IMAGE WITH MATHEMATICS

One can obtain a great deal of information about an image, such as whether an image is real or virtual, reduced or magnified, and inverted or upright, by drawing a ray diagram. If the ray diagram is drawn to scale (i.e., the measurements on the page relate to the true measurements of the situation in some way), one can also calculate the exact height of the image and its distance from the mirror. However, ray diagrams are not usually the most efficient way to calculate the height and distance of an image from the mirror. Small mistakes in measurements can cause a large distortion in values when the measurements are scaled down to fit on a piece of paper. In most situations in which these values are necessary, the mirror equation or the magnification equation should be used, as follows:

Mirror Equation

$$\frac{1}{f} = \frac{1}{d_o} + \frac{1}{d_i}$$

Magnification Equation

$$M = \frac{h_i}{h_o} = -\frac{d_i}{d_o}$$

For these equations, f is the focal length (the distance to the focal point), d is the image's distance from the mirror, h is the image's height, and M is magnification. A subscript i is used to indicate that the measurement is for the image, whereas the subscript o indicates that the value is for the object. All the measurements must in the same units except for magnification, which is a unit-

+/– Sign Conventions for Mirror and Magnification Equations		
SYMBOL	**+ OR –**	**THIS MEANS THAT. . .**
f	+	The mirror is concave.
	–	The mirror is convex.
d_i	+	The image is in front of the mirror and is a real image.
	–	The image appears to be behind the mirror and is a virtual image.
h_i	+	The image is upright.
	–	The image is inverted.

less ratio. A magnification of 2 indicates that the image is twice the size of the object, whereas a magnification of 0.5 indicates that the image is half the size of the object. The above table explains the positive and negative sign conventions for these equations and what these signs convey about the mirror or image or both.

USES OF MIRRORS

Mirrors are so integrated in our everyday lives that they are all but unnoticed until they are needed. The most common use for mirrors is for vanity—people can view themselves in a mirror and see how they look. A plane mirror is most typically used for this purpose, although occasionally a slightly concave mirror is used, for example, for the application of makeup, to provide a more detailed view. Dentists also use a magnifying mirror of this type to be able to view places in a patient's mouth that are hard to reach. A convex mirror is frequently used whenever a wider field of vision is needed, such as on side mirrors on a car and for security measures in the corner of a store. A convex mirror placed in the corner of a store allows employees to keep watch over a larger section of the store than would otherwise be possible.

Reflecting telescopes were designed in the 17th century to correct some of the problems that occurred with previously created telescopes. The many different types of reflecting telescopes all start with a concave primary mirror at the end of the telescope tube. Light enters the far end of the tube and reflects off the concave mirror to converge at a point within the tube. Different types of reflecting telescopes use diverse methods to get these focused light rays from inside of the tube to an eyepiece for easy viewing. The Gregorian design, which Scottish astronomer James Gregory (1638–75) first wrote about in 1663, uses a smaller, concave secondary mirror to reflect the light out through a small hole within the primary mirror. The upright and magnified image that the concave mirror creates makes this telescope popular for viewing objects on Earth.

The Newtonian telescope, built in 1668 by British physicist Sir Isaac Newton (1643–1727), was the first successful reflecting telescope built, although it was designed after the Gregorian telescope. The secondary mirror in a Newtonian telescope is a plane mirror that is placed at a 45° angle; this mirror directs the light rays to an eyepiece placed in the side of the tube. The telescope is impractical for viewing objects on Earth because it produces an inverted image; however, having only one piece of curved mirror makes this telescope easier and cheaper to produce and, thus, popular with amateur astronomers.

Convex mirrors are often used for security reasons because they reduce the image and allow more of a room to be visible than it would in either a plane or concave mirror. (Courtesy of Visionmetaizers.com)

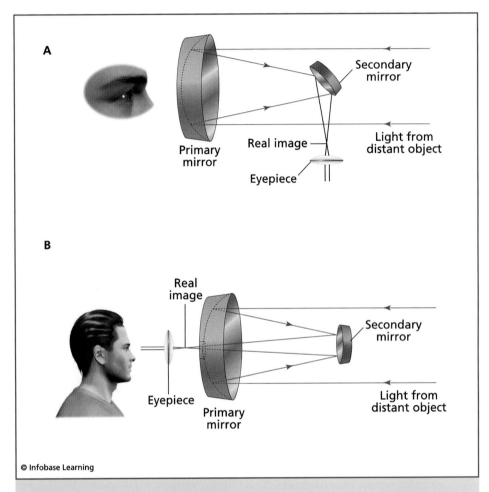

The mirrors in a reflecting telescope are used to focus light and send it out the side to an eyepiece (a) or through a hole in the primary mirror (b).

The Cassegrain telescope, designed in 1672, was attributed to Laurent Cassegrain (1629–93), a French priest, although the debate continues as to whether this man designed the telescope or whether it was another man with the same last name. The Cassegrain telescope has a convex secondary mirror that reflects the focused light back down the tube and out through a hole in the primary mirror, similarly to the Gregorian telescope. The advantage to this telescope is that the tube length can be significantly shorter than those of other telescopes. Many variations of this type of telescope exist. This design is also used in many radio telescopes.

Mirrors are used in some film cameras to redirect light rays to a viewing point for the photographer. In simple "point and shoot" cameras, the photographer looks through a transparent viewfinder to see an image close to the one that will be recorded on film. With a single lens reflex camera, the viewfinder shows the actual image that will appear on the film. A small, flat mirror placed between the lens and the film redirects the light rays to a prism or second mirror to turn the image upright and then to the viewfinder. When the photographer pushes the button, the mirror is moved out of the way so that the light rays hit the film. This process causes the image in the viewfinder to go dark while the picture is being taken.

SUMMARY

The law of reflection determines the angle at which light is reflected off of a surface. According to this law, the angle between the incoming light ray and the normal (a line that is perpendicular to the surface at that point) and the angle between the reflecting light ray and the normal are the same. All the incoming light rays are reflected at the same angle from a smooth surface and create a clear reflection called a specular reflection. The normal of a rough surface is in a different direction for every incident light ray. The uneven surface scatters the reflected rays, creating a diffuse reflection.

A mirror is any surface that creates a specular reflection, although modern mirrors are typically glass with a coating of tin or silver on the back. Images created by mirrors can be classified in several different ways. They can be real or virtual, depending on whether the light rays actually meet at the point where the image is formed or whether they only appear to do so. Images can also be upright or inverted compared to the original object or reduced in size or magnified. There are three types of mirrors—plane, concave, and convex—whose differences involve the shape of the mirror and the type of image formed by the mirror. A plane mirror has a flat surface and creates a virtual image that is upright and unchanged in size compared to the object.

A concave mirror has a surface that curves inward, causing reflected light to converge at the focal point of the mirror. The focal point of a mirror is always one-half the distance to the center of curvature of that mirror. A concave mirror can create many different types of images, depending on how far the object is located in front of the mirror. When the object is between the mirror and the focal point, the image is virtual, upright, and magnified. When the object is between the focal point and the center of curvature, the image is real, inverted, and magnified. When the object is behind the center of curvature, the image is real, inverted, and reduced in size. A convex mirror has a surface that curves outward and is sometimes called a *diverging mirror* because it causes reflected light rays to spread out. This kind of mirror always makes an image that is virtual, upright, and reduced in size no matter where the object is located.

Ray diagrams can be drawn for concave and convex mirrors to visualize the image. Three rays are always drawn in these diagrams from the top of the object to where the top of the object would appear in an image. When virtual images are formed, reflected rays must be traced back to where they seem to be coming from. In addition, two equations—the mirror equation and the magnification equation—can be used to calculate the exact location and size of an image formed. Locating images is important when using mirrors so that the light rays are focused on the correct spot.

A plane mirror can be used, for example, as a bathroom fixture, a decoration in homes, and a child's toy. It also be used to reflect an image to the viewfinder in some types of film cameras and in the simplest type of reflecting telescope. A concave mirror is frequently used when magnification is needed, such as in the mirrors that a dentist uses to view teeth and in the mirrors that people use to apply makeup. A convex mirror is used when a reduced image is required to provide a wider view, such as in side mirrors for cars and in security mirrors in stores.

Understanding how mirrors work is important because they are so common in our modern world. This knowledge should include an understanding of why a reflection is made or not made, where that reflected image will appear, and whether that image will be large or small. Understanding the ways in which mirrors are used helps explain objects in the world.

6

Refraction and Lenses

Chapter 6 focuses on what happens when light passes through an object instead of bouncing off it. The chapter uses Snell's law to explain the way in which light bends as it passes through different materials and the effect that this has on how objects appear. The chapter continues by discussing the two most common types of simple lenses—convex and concave—including what types of images they form. The chapter also examines equations that allow one to locate and describe images mathematically. Finally, it discusses some of the many uses for lenses.

SNELL'S LAW

When electromagnetic waves, such as visible light, travel through a medium, they are constantly absorbed by the particles of that medium and then reemitted as a new electromagnetic wave. For this reason, light travels the fastest through a vacuum at 9.8 x 10^8 feet per second (3.0 x 10^8 m per second) because there are no particles to absorb and remit the light. Some mediums require more time for this absorption and emission than others do. The rate at which a medium achieves this is called its **optical density**.

Light travels slowest through mediums that are optically dense, such as diamonds, and fastest in mediums that are less optically dense, such as air.

A quantitative indicator of optical density is a material's **index of refraction**, which is represented by the symbol n. The index of refraction for a material shows how many times slower light travels in that material than it does in a vacuum. The equation used to calculate the index of refraction is as follows:

$$n_{material} = \frac{c}{v_{material}},$$

where c is equal to the speed of light in a vacuum, 9.8×10^8 feet per second (3.0×10^8 meters per second). An index of refraction value of 2 for a substance means that light moves twice as slow in that substance versus in a vacuum. There are no index of refraction values less than 1 because light moves fastest in a vacuum. The following table shows some sample indices of refraction.

As light waves pass from one medium to another they bend because of this change in speed; this bending is called **refraction**.

Indices of Refraction for Some Materials	
MATERIAL	**INDEX OF REFRACTION**
Vacuum	1.0000
Air	1.0003
Ice	1.309
Water	1.333
Crown Glass	1.52
Zircon	1.923
Diamond	2.417

Light reflecting from the straw is refracted as it moves from water to air, causing the straw to appear broken. (Courtesy of the Department of Theory and Advanced Computation, University of Surrey)

Imagine a person riding a lawnmower along the sidewalk and then turning it onto the grass. As the lawnmower enters the grass area where it must move slower, its path changes as one wheel of the lawnmower changes mediums before the others do. The same is true for light waves, as they move from a medium with a low index of refraction to one with a higher index of refraction, the light waves bend toward the normal. When light waves move from a slower medium to a faster—high index of refraction to lower— they bend away from the normal.

This bending can be seen when reaching for an object in the bottom of a tub full of water. The light rays reflecting off the object bend as they pass from the water to the air; reaching for the object where it appears to be results in grabbing nothing but water. **Snell's law**, or the law of refraction, helps determine how much a light ray bends as it changes mediums. Snell's law is named for Dutch mathematician Willebrord Snel (1580–1626) who conceived it in 1621 but did not publish it within his lifetime. However, the law of refraction was first described in 984 by Ibn Sahl (940–1000), the Arabian physicist. He made use of the equation to find the shape of a lens that was able to focus light into a sharp point. The equation is sometimes called the Snell-Descartes law in honor of René Descartes (1596–1650), the French physicist who explained the law in a 1637 paper.

Snell's law uses the indices of refraction for both materials to show a relationship between the angle of incidence, θ_i, and the angle of refraction, θ_r. These angles are both measured from the normal, the line perpendicular to the surface at the point where the light strikes. The following equation of Snell's law can be used to calculate unknown indices of refraction, or the angle at which a light ray approaches or leaves a change in medium:

$$n_i \sin\theta_i = n_r \sin\theta_r$$

Willebrord Snel was a mathematician who is credited with the discovery of the law of refraction. This law later became known as Snell's law.
(Courtesy of Wikipedia)

When a light ray travels from a medium with a high index of refraction to a medium with a low index of refraction, the refracted ray bends away from the normal. As the angle of incidence increases (i.e., the incoming light ray moves away from the normal), so does the angle of refraction. Eventually, the angle of incidence reaches the critical angle, and the angle of refraction becomes

Overcoming Refraction to Catch Fish

Many animals, like bears and some birds, catch fish to eat by grabbing them out of the water with their paws, mouths, or beaks. Humans often spearfish or bowfish in a similar manner by standing in shallow water or on shore and by striking a fish with a spear or arrow. This method is harder than it looks because not only does a hunter need to be faster than the fish, but also the fish is not where it appears to be because of refraction. Fish and other underwater creatures appear to be further away and closer to the surface to those preying on them above the water's surface. As the reflected light rays leave the fish, they travel from the water and enter the air. Because the air has a lower index of refraction, the light rays bend away from the normal, making it seem that the light rays come from further back and somewhat higher up in the water. How far displaced the actual fish is from the location where it appears to be depends on the angle at which the hunter is looking into the water. The closer the hunter is to looking straight down (i.e., when there is no refraction at all), the closer the actual fish will be to where the hunter thinks it is located.

Hunters, both human and animal, can learn to adjust for this refraction by aiming lower and deeper, which takes patience and practice. Some bears will put their faces under the water while hunting to rid themselves of refraction altogether, or they will walk in the water to hunt directly underneath them. When the line of sight is perpendicular to the water, no refraction occurs because the incidence angle is zero and thus the refraction angle is also zero.

greater than 90°—that is, that the ray is completely reflected back into the original medium in a process called **total internal reflection**. The critical angle is different depending on the medium that the light ray travels through and typically is only useful in materials that have a high optical density. Fiber optic cables use total internal reflection to bounce a signal carrying light wave down a plastic wire. These plastic wires are much smaller, lighter, and more durable than metal wires. Properly cut diamonds are shaped so that total internal reflection of light is created within the stone, causing them to sparkle.

WHAT IS A LENS?

A lens is a material, usually glass or plastic, that refracts light as it is transmitted. Most common lenses have the same curve on each side of the lens, although a lens can be curved on one side and flat on the other or even have different degrees of curvature on either side of the lens. In most cases, lenses are considered to be thin lenses—that is, they are thin enough so that the light rays can be considered as only bending once as they leave the lens and enter the air. In reality, the light rays refract as they leave the air and enter the lens; however, when the lens is thin, the light rays almost immediately change direction again as they leave the lens.

Like with mirrors, lenses also have focal points where they either focus light or appear to focus light. Uniquely, a lens has two focal points (one on either side of the lens) because light can pass through a lens in either direction. A converging lens causes light rays to bend toward the focal point as the rays are refracted. A diverging lens causes light rays to bend away from each other so that they appear to originate from the focal point on the far side of the lens. The focal length of a lens is determined by the index of refraction of the lens, the curvature of the lens, and the medium that the lens is placed in.

CONVEX LENSES

A **convex lens** is a lens that curves outward. For the purposes of this chapter, the term will specifically be used to refer to double convex lens. A double convex lens has symmetrical outwardly curving sides. This type of lens is also sometimes called a *converging lens* because it typically causes refracted rays to meet at the

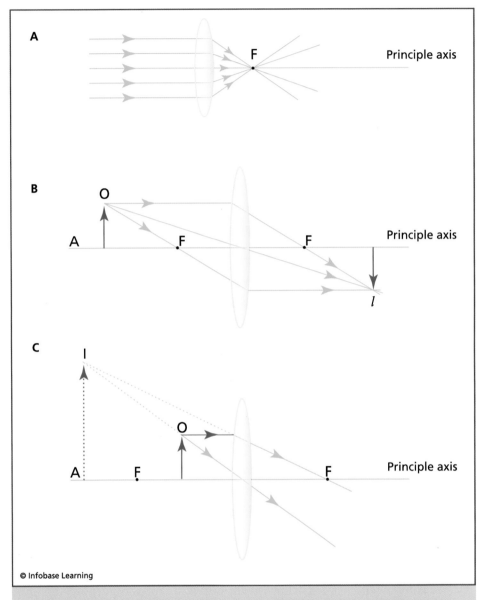

(a) A convex lens causes light rays to converge at the focal point, F. (b) When the object, O, is placed beyond the focal point, the image, I, is real and inverted. It can be reduced or magnified depending on how far the object is located beyond the focal point. (c) When the object, O, is placed between the focal point and the lens, a virtual, upright, and magnified image, I, is produced.

focal point. A convex lens can produce different types of images depending on the location of the object. When the object is far from the lens (at least twice the focal length), the image produced is real, inverted, and reduced in size. When the object is beyond the focal point but less than twice the focal length away from the lens, the image produced is real, inverted, and magnified. Real images such as these can be projected onto a surface, like when focusing the Sun's light into a bright point on a sheet of paper. When the object is very close to the lens, a virtual, upright, and magnified image is produced, which is the type of image produced when using a magnifying glass.

Ray diagrams can be drawn for a convex lens to locate where an image will be produced and to determine what that image will look like. The rays drawn are somewhat similar to those drawn for mirror ray diagrams except that they pass through the lens instead of reflecting off it. Three rays are drawn whenever possible, although only two are required to locate an image. The table below lists details about the three rays that are most commonly drawn for a convex lens.

When the object is between the lens and the focal point, the second ray cannot be drawn. A light ray cannot leave the top of the object and travel through the focal point and the lens without

Ray Diagram for a Convex Lens

RAY	RAY ORIENTATION	RAY MOVEMENT
1	Parallel to the principal axis	This ray starts parallel to the principal axis and then passes through the focal point, F, on the far side of the lens.
2	Ray traveling through the focal point	This ray travels toward the focal point, F, on the near side of the lens and travels parallel to the principal axis after refraction.
3	Ray refracts on the same path	This ray travels through the center of the lens without any noticeable bending.

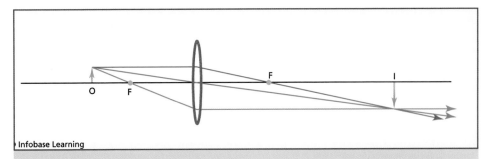

Infobase Learning

Ray 1 (red arrow), Ray 2 (green arrow), and Ray 3 (blue arrow) are refracted and meet to form a real, inverted, and slightly magnified image, I.

bending so that ray is omitted in these cases. When drawn, Rays 1 and 3 do not clearly ever really intersect and create a real image; therefore, these rays must be traced back to where they appear to originate in order to find a virtual image.

CONCAVE LENSES

A **concave lens** is a lens with one or two sides that curve outward, although this type of lens used in this book will mean a double

Ray Diagram for a Concave Lens		
RAY	**RAY ORIENTATION**	**RAY MOVEMENT**
1	Parallel to the principal axis	This ray starts parallel to the principal axis and refracts away from the principal axis so that the refracted ray appears to originate from the focal point, *F*, on the near side of the lens.
2	Ray traveling through the focal point	This ray travels toward the focal point, *F*, on the far side of the lens and is refracted so that it travels parallel to the principal axis.
3	Ray refracts on the same path	This ray travels through the center of the lens without any noticeable bending.

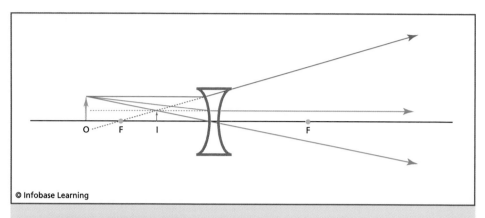

© Infobase Learning

Ray 1 (red arrow), Ray 2 (green arrow), and Ray 3 (blue arrow) are refracted away from each other and form an image, I, that is virtual, upright, and reduced in size.

concave lens—one that has two sides that curve outward identi-cally. A concave lens has two focal points, one on either side of the lens. A concave lens can also be called a *diverging lens* because its curvature causes the light rays to bend away from each other after refraction. The light rays do not really meet on the far side of the lens; therefore, images always appear where the light rays appear to meet on the same side of the lens as the object. Images created by a concave lens are always virtual, upright, and reduced in size, as shown in the figure above.

Ray diagrams for concave lenses are very similar to those drawn for convex lenses; however, the light rays must always be traced back to where they appear to originate. The table on the bottom of page 86 lists details about the three rays that are drawn to locate and describe an image formed by a concave lens. All three rays can be drawn in any situation.

LOCATING AN IMAGE WITH MATHEMATICS

Although drawing a ray diagram gives a great deal of information about the image formed, sometimes using equations to calculate how far away an image is located and its height and to determine whether the image is real or virtual and upright or inverted is more efficient and allows for more precise values. If the lens is a thin lens, then the thin lens equation and the magnification equation used with mirrors can be used as follows:

Thin Lens Equation

$$\frac{1}{f} = \frac{1}{d_o} + \frac{1}{d_i}$$

Magnification Equation

$$M = \frac{h_i}{h_o} = -\frac{d_i}{d_o}$$

These equations are identical to those used for mirrors, as described in chapter 5, although the mirror equation is now called the *thin lens equation*. In these equations, the subscript "*o*" indicates that the measurement refers to the object, whereas the subscript "*i*" indicates that the measurement refers to the image. The symbol *f* represents the focal length—the distance to the focal point. *M* is the magnification of the lens—how many times larger the image is compared to the object. The symbol *d* is used to indicate the distance from the lens, and the symbol *h* indicates the height of the object or image.

The positive and negative sign conventions for these equations are almost identical to those for the equations used for mirrors; a positive image height indicates the image is upright, and a negative height indicates the image is inverted. In addition, a positive image distance means that the image is on the far side of the lens and real, whereas a negative distance indicates that the image is on the near side of the lens and virtual. One difference is that a positive focal length for lenses indicates that the lens is convex, and a negative value indicates that the lens is concave.

USES OF LENSES

As early as 424 B.C.E., lenses were being used as simple magnifying glasses. When a convex lens is placed close to an object so that the object is within the focal length, the object becomes magnified. This basic idea of a convex lens magnifying an object is still one of the most common uses of lenses in items such as telescopes and microscopes. A convex lens is also used for the real images it can project onto a surface in movie theaters and classrooms. Although less commonly used, a concave lens still has a place in some cameras and telescopes. Both types of lenses can be used in eyeglasses to correct vision problems.

Convex lenses had been used to magnify things for years. In 1608, two Dutch spectacle makers, Hans Lippershey (1570–1619) and Zacharias Jansen (1580–1638), designed the first refracting telescope. However, Galileo Galilei (1564–1642), the Italian astronomer and physicist, frequently gets credit for refining and creating the first useful refracting telescope. His telescope was built in 1609 and was the first to be designed for celestial observations. The Galilean telescope uses a convex lens to focus the light rays and a concave lens for the eyepiece to produce an upright image. Galileo's best telescopes could magnify objects by as much as 30 times their original size. In 1611, German astronomer Johannes Kepler (1571–1630) improved Galileo's design by using a convex lens for the eyepiece instead. This Keplerian telescope allows for a wider field of view and can produce higher magnifications, but it produces an inverted image. Although refracting telescopes are still used in items like binoculars, they have largely been replaced by reflecting telescopes. Refracting telescopes suffer from chromatic aberration in which not all wavelengths of light are focused at the same place because of different degrees of refraction, thus causing fringes of color along color boundaries and unclear images.

Originally, the lens used in a camera was a single convex lens that focused a real image on the film in the camera body. Using a single lens, however, offered no way to correct distortions like

Camera lenses contain a mixture of convex and concave lenses. Focusing a camera is accomplished by adjusting the focal length, which focuses the image at different distances. (Courtesy of Canon)

chromatic aberration. A modern camera lens is a compound lens— several different lenses made of different materials that work together to produce as perfect an image as is possible. Figuring out how to make each part of the compound lens work together to correct optical aberrations caused by other lenses is not an easy task. A good lens can be twice as expensive as the camera body itself. Professional cameras have detachable lenses that allow photographers to change their camera lenses for specific tasks. The differences in these lenses are primarily related to the range of focal lengths for the lens. The longer the focal length of a lens, the greater the magnification of the produced image and the narrower the field of view that the lens offers.

Eyeglasses for Common Vision Problems

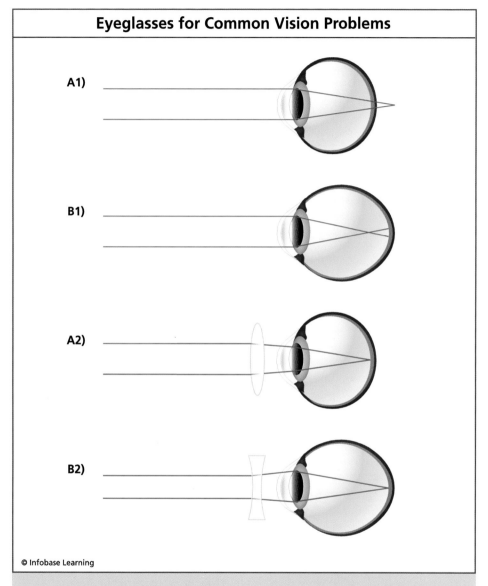

A1)

B1)

A2)

B2)

For a farsighted person (a1), the light rays meet too far back, whereas for a nearsighted person (b1), the rays meet too far forward. A convex lens is used to correct farsightedness (a2), and a concave lens is used to correct nearsightedness (b2).

Many people are thankful for the use of lenses in eyeglasses to correct vision problems. The lenses in the eye are supposed to focus incoming light rays onto the retina in the back of the eye; however, sometimes light is focused incorrectly. When the light is focused too early the person suffers from myopia, or nearsightedness. For this person, near objects will be clearly focused, but items at a distance will seem blurry. Nearsightedness can be corrected with a concave lens, which allows the light rays from distant objects to be properly focused on the retina. In some cases, the focal point within a person's eye is too far back and they suffer from hyperopia, or farsightedness—near objects are blurry while those further away are clearly focused. A convex lens is used to bring the focal length for near objects into place on the retina. A cylindrical lens is used to correct astigmatism, whereby incoming light rays cannot focus into a point usually because of an irregular curvature of the eye,. A cylindrical lens can be either concave or convex; however, instead of focusing incoming light rays into a point, this type of lens focuses them into a line.

SUMMARY

When light rays move through a medium they must be absorbed and then reemitted by the particles that they are traveling through. Materials absorb and reemit light rays at different rates, which is why light travels at different speeds in different mediums. This property can be described by a material's index of refraction, whereby the higher the value, the slower light moves in that substance. As light rays move from one medium to another, they bend because of their change in speed, which is called refraction. If the light rays speed up in the new medium, they bend away from the normal; if they slow down, they bend toward the normal. Snell's law helps calculate how much the light ray bends during refraction through the relationship between the incidence angle and the indices of refraction for both mediums. In cases where the increase in speed is particularly great, total internal reflection can occur. Total internal reflection happens when the incident angle passes a critical angle and when the angle of refraction becomes greater than 90°, causing the light rays to be reflected back within the same medium.

A lens is a material that refracts light as it transmits it, thus causing it to either converge or diverge. A converging lens is called a convex lens and curves outward. A concave lens with inward curving sides causes light to diverge as it is refracted. Lenses typically have a focal point on either side of the lens whose position is determined by the lens material and the curvature of the lens. Using and studying thin lenses that only noticeably bend light as the light exits the lens and enters the medium surrounding it is most practical.

Ray diagrams can be drawn for both types of lenses to locate and describe the image that they form. A convex lens forms an image that is inverted and real when the object is placed beyond the focal length. This image can be reduced or magnified, depending on how far from the lens the object is placed. These real images are used when movies are projected onto a screen in a movie theater or when a teacher uses a data projector in a classroom. If the object is placed closer to the lens than the focal length, a virtual, upright, and magnified image is produced, such as that produced by a magnifying glass. A concave lens always produces an image that is virtual, upright, and reduced in size, regardless of where the object is placed. Thin lens and magnification equations can be used to calculate the values of image distance, height, and magnification for either type of lens.

A convex lens is the most commonly used lens because it can magnify objects that are close and because it can produce real images of objects that are further away. A convex lens is used in refracting telescopes, camera lenses, projectors, microscopes, and eyeglasses to correct vision problems like farsightedness. A concave lens is used in some refraction telescopes, camera lenses, and eyeglasses for people with nearsightedness.

Because lenses are such an important part of our modern world, understanding what they are and how they work is important. Lenses have many similarities to mirrors (e.g., lenses can be converging or diverging); however, instead of bouncing light rays off themselves, lenses transmit them and bend the rays as they pass through. Understanding how light behaves when it passes through a substance is vital to understanding some of what is being seen. For example, a pencil appears broken in a half-full glass of water when it is viewed from the side. This phenomenon, and others like it, cannot be explained without an understanding of refraction and lenses.

Interference and Diffraction

Chapter 7 focuses on two last types of wave interactions—interference and diffraction. Interference occurs when two waves meet each other, and diffraction occurs when waves move through an opening or around an obstacle. The chapter goes on to discuss the many ways these two interactions are used, including how some musical instruments produce sound.

INTERFERENCE

Waves move away from their source in all directions so that the waves never interfere with each other under normal circumstances. Obstacles, openings, and even other wave sources, however, can cause waves to interact with each other. Dutch physicist Christiaan Huygens (1629–95) was the first to suggest that light behaves as a wave. His principle of superposition states that each point in a wave front can be viewed as the source of secondary waves that will move away from it. These secondary waves move away from the original wave in all directions and add up to continue the primary wave. This principle is used to simplify wave propagation and motion and to explain behavior such as reflection and refraction. The principle also explains that when two waves interact with each other, the resulting wave has a displacement, or amplitude, equal to the sum of the displacement of the original two waves at that point.

Wave interference can result in a larger wave, **constructive interference**, or a smaller wave, **destructive interference**. When two identical waves line up in phase—that is, their crests and troughs, or compressions and rarefactions, line up with one another, the resulting wave has an amplitude that is double that of either original wave. The wave has crests and troughs that are twice as high and twice as low, respectively, as those of either original wave. Two waves with the same wavelengths completely cancel each other out when the waves line up with one another in such a manner whereby the crest of one wave meets up with the trough of the other—or a compression meets up with a rarefaction. When two waves with different wavelengths interfere with each other, the amplitudes of the original waves are added to produce the amplitude of the resulting wave. In this case, the amplitude of a wave at the crests or compression is positive, whereas the amplitude of a wave at the troughs or rarefaction is negative.

Constructive and destructive interference can occur with any type of wave, but they will not occur if waves are not present—a fact that British physicist Thomas Young (1773–1829) used in the early 19th century to prove that light had a wave nature. Young's double slit experiment showed that light passed through two small slits produces light and dark bands on a screen because of constructive and destructive interference of the light waves. This experimental step was the first of its kind to prove the dual nature of light.

DIFFRACTION

When water waves strike the legs of a pier, they curve around the obstacle. When the waves pass through an opening in a jetty, they bend as well. This bending of waves around obstacles or through openings is **diffraction**. Diffraction is why voices can be heard from a classroom by a listener who walks past the room, even

Diffraction causes these surface waves to bend as they pass around the point of land. (Courtesy of Jim Pell)

when the person is not directly in front of the door. The sound waves of the speakers' voices bend as the waves pass through the doorway and move down the hallway in either direction. The sound waves appear to originate from the doorway to the person in the hallway.

The first statement of Huygens' principle of superposition is important in understanding why waves undergo diffraction. Each point on the wave front is the source of the secondary waves emitted in a circular fashion. The obstacle or sides of the opening block some of these secondary waves from adding to the others and produce a curved pattern. This principle also explains why the sound waves from a room seem to originate from the doorway because secondary waves did originate from wave fronts in the doorway. All waves can undergo diffraction; however, diffraction is more noticeable in some waves than it is in others. When a man stands in the Sun and looks at his shadow, the light from the Sun has not diffracted enough around the edges of his body to fill in

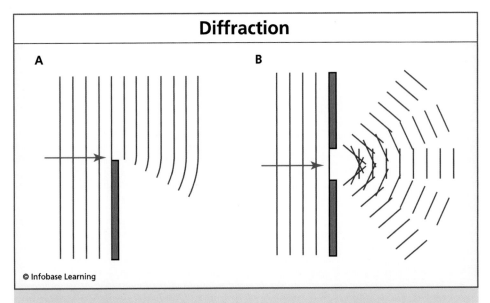

Diffraction

A

B

© Infobase Learning

When waves pass around an obstacle (a), they bend around that obstacle. When they pass through an opening (b), they bend and create a circular pattern. These are both examples of diffraction.

his shadow, but it has diffracted enough to make the edges of his shadow appear blurry. Longer wavelengths undergo a sharper diffraction, or bending; in addition, the smaller the opening, the greater the diffraction that occurs. Diffraction is not significant if the obstacle or opening is greater in length than the wavelength of the incoming wave. The very small wavelength of light is why its diffraction is so much less than that of sound waves moving around most everyday obstacles. For example, when walking down a hallway towards an open classroom, sounds from the room reach a person much sooner than light does, because the sound waves diffract much further.

A diffraction grating takes advantage of the variations in the amount of diffraction for different wavelengths of light. A diffraction grating has ridges or obstacles at evenly spaced intervals that cause light waves to disperse into their component colors based on their different wavelengths. This grating produces a rainbow of light, similar to what a person sees when light shines off the back of a compact disc, whereby the grooves on the back act like a diffraction grating. Because the different colors of light diffract in different directions, some colors from adjoining ridges interact and cause constructive and destructive interference.

USING INTERFERENCE AND DIFFRACTION

The rainbow of colors that are visible on a soap bubble or in a puddle of oil are examples of thin-film interference. Thin-film interference occurs when light strikes the surface of the film, some rays are reflected and some are transmitted. As those rays that were transmitted reach the bottom surface of the film, they are again reflected or transmitted. This process produces two sets of reflected rays, one from the top surface and one from the bottom, that produce constructive and destructive interference with each other. In addition, refraction has dispersed the light during its transitions into and out of the film; this dispersion of light causes the swirling patterns of color. The color and the spacing of the bands of color can be used to measure the thickness of the film, which is useful when the film is too thin to be measured by conventional methods. Thin-film interference is a method that is used to create coatings on camera lenses or glasses to filter out specific colors through destructive interference. This type of interference is what causes the iridescent colors of some bird feathers, like on peacocks, and butterfly wings.

Interference of sound waves can occur anytime that two sources of sound, like speakers, produce overlapping waves. When designing a theater or a concert hall, such as Carnegie Hall in New York City, engineers must consider the interference of sound waves and the resulting influence on sound propagation. Reflected sound waves must not cause destructive interference and deaden the sound. The placement of two or more speakers in a home theater can cause interference. Constructive interference is purposefully created, hopefully directed at the seating area; how-

(continues on page 102)

Holograms

A hologram is a three-dimensional image of a real object created by a two-dimensional surface. Holograms preserve the light reflected off an object and reproduce these light rays so convincingly that the object itself can seem to appear instead of just an image of it. Holograms can range from a simple sticker on a product or credit card to prevent forgery to a complex rendering of an object with or without apparent movement. The first hologram was created in 1947 by Hungarian-British engineer Dennis Gabor (1900–79) who discovered holography by chance while trying to improve the function of electron microscopes. The hologram did not become practical or commonly used until the development of the laser in 1960.

Holograms are typically created with monochromatic laser light—light that has all the same wavelength and color and that travels with all the light waves lined up crest to crest and trough to trough. This type of coherent light is what makes laser light so bright and its light beams so cohesive. A beam splitter is used to split a pulse of laser light into two light beams. One beam, the reference beam, is bounced off of a mirror and sent through a diverging lens to spread out the beam before it strikes the surface of the holographic film. (Holographic film is similar to photographic film, but it has a finer grain and responds to even tinier changes in light.) At the same time, the second beam, the object beam, is sent through a diverging lens, bounced off a mirror, and reflected off the object before striking the holographic film simultaneously with the reference beam. The film effectively records the interference of the two light beams, creating inference fringes on the film that act as a diffraction grating. The object beam is created as the same monochromatic light shines on the film, thus making the object appear to be within the film like the virtual images created by a mirror.

There are two types of holograms—transmission holograms and reflection holograms. In a transmission hologram, light must be shone through the holographic film to create the three-dimensional image, whereas a reflection hologram only needs to have light reflected off its surface. Rainbow holograms can be shown without the use of laser light, thus allowing for the more practical use of white light to create images. A hologram image

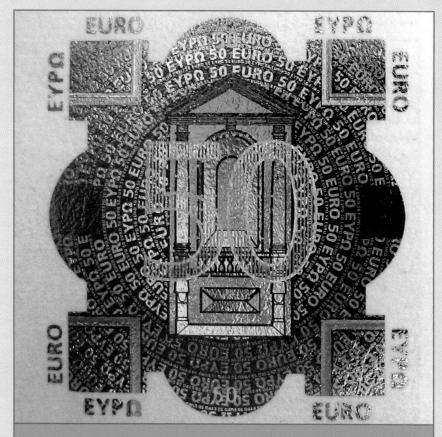

Holograms are frequently used for security to prevent replication such as on this 50 Euros bill. (Courtesy of Hëike Lochel)

can appear to move by creating multiple images on the same film with the object in different positions. The image may be visually different depending on the angle between the viewer and the hologram. In addition, relative motion can cause the image to change. Although the image itself does not move, the rapid change from one image to another can make the image appear to be in motion.

(continued from page 99)

ever, destructive interference is typically also created, which explains why some parts of the room may seem quieter than others. Noise-cancelling headphones have a microphone that receives the ambient sound (i.e., sound in the immediate or surrounding area). This microphone allows the headphones to produce a similar wave that creates destructive interference, thus effectively reducing or eliminating the unwanted sound.

Animals such as owls and elephants use diffraction to aid group communication. Owls and other birds emit long-wavelength sound waves as low-pitched hoots that allow the waves to be diffracted around tree trunks and to carry further through the woods. Elephants travel in large herds that may be spread out miles from beginning to end. They use infrasonic waves to communicate their movements along the herd, whether members of the herd are within site of one another or not. The long wavelength of these sounds allows them to travel over many miles, thus allowing these herds to synchronize their movements.

Like a prism, diffraction gratings can be used to divide any light into its individual colors but with higher resolution than that of a prism. When atoms absorb energy, the energy is quickly released as light. Because atoms of each element are unique, the light that they produce is also unique. Diffraction gratings are often used to separate the light emitted by an unknown compound to identify the elements within that compound by the colors of light it emits.

STANDING WAVES AND MUSICAL INSTRUMENTS

When a mechanical wave is confined to a limited space, such as a rope tied to a doorknob, the regular repeating pattern of crests and troughs is no longer evident. If a person vibrates the end of the rope to send wave pulses down its length, most of the energy of the wave is reflected at the end of the rope, creating waves traveling in the opposite direction. These waves interfere with each other, disrupting the orderly pattern of crests and troughs. However, if the waves are generated at precisely the right frequency,

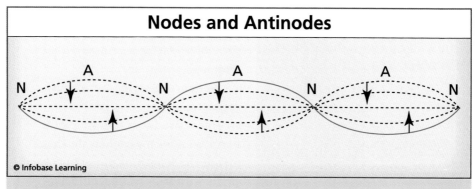

Nodes and Antinodes

© Infobase Learning

A standing wave is characterized by nodes, N, that appear to be standing still and by antinodes, A, that are the areas of greatest displacement.

this interference can cause a wave pattern, called a **standing wave**, in which parts of the wave appear to be standing still. The points along the medium that appear to be standing still are the **nodes** of the standing wave. **Antinodes** are the areas of greatest displacement in between the nodes; these areas continuously switch from a crest to a trough and back again. The nodes of a standing wave are portions where the two waves produce complete destructive interference, whereas the antinodes occur when the two waves interfere constructively.

Because the wavelength of the standing wave pattern is specifically related to the length of the medium available, specific frequencies of waves must be used to create this type of pattern in a given medium. There are multiple frequencies that will work to create a standing wave pattern for each medium, which create waves that differ in the number of nodes and antinodes. The simplest pattern that can be produced in a given medium is called the *first harmonic*. This wave has two nodes that remain stationary, and one antinode that continuously changes from a crest to a trough. The wavelength of this standing wave is twice the length of the medium because only one-half of the wave exists at a time. The second harmonic has three nodes and two antinodes with a wavelength that is exactly the length of the medium. For each

Playing a clarinet creates a standing wave along the length of the instrument. Pressing different keys varies the frequency of the standing wave. (Courtesy of Harry Goldson)

new harmonic, the wavelength of the new wave is halved, and the wave pattern gains another node and antinode.

When the string on a musical instrument is plucked, the instrument produces standing wave harmonics with wavelengths that match the length of the string. A single vibrating string on a violin can produce several harmonics at the same time to create a rich and full sound. Violinists can change the pitch on their instruments by placing a finger on the string to shorten its length and change the frequency of the wave produced. Standing waves also occur for longitudinal waves in wind instruments. The column of air inside the body of a wind instrument acts as the medium with a fixed length, even if one end of the column is open. Pressing keys along the column's length changes the frequency of the standing waves produced by the instrument by changing the length of the column of air.

SUMMARY

When waves interact with each other, they can make a larger or a smaller wave through constructive and destructive interference, depending on which parts of the waves overlap. When two crests or two troughs meet, the amplitude of the wave increases, thus creating a larger wave. When a crest and a trough interact they produce a smaller wave because the amplitude decreases. When light shines through a thin film of oil or soap, some rays are reflected at the top and bottom edges of the film. When these reflected rays meet they interfere with each other and cause patterns of color along with bright and dark spots. Thin-film interference is a method used in coatings to block specific colors of light through destructive interference. Music halls or home theatres also use the interference of sound waves to increase sound-wave propagation.

Diffraction occurs when waves bend around an obstacle or through an opening, such as when a person hears a marching band despite being outside of the stadium where the band plays. However, the person will most likely only hear drums and other lower-pitched instruments because low-frequency and longer-wavelength waves diffract the most. A diffraction grating has several evenly spaced grooves or ridges along its length. Light diffracts when it strikes these obstacles; however, because the colors of light have different wavelengths, each color diffracts a different amount, thus causing the light to be dispersed into its component colors. Diffraction gratings exist on the back of compact discs and are frequently used to identify the different colors in a light source.

Standing waves are caused when the reflection of a wave interferes with itself, causing both constructive and destructive interference. This interference occurs when a wave travels in a medium with a fixed length. Nodes are points on a standing wave pattern in which the medium appears to be stationary and are caused by destructive interference. Antinodes are the points of greatest displacement in which the wave alternates between being a crest and a trough and are caused by constructive interference. The manipulation of this type of wave pattern is how string and wind instruments produce their sounds.

Waves are constantly in motion in the world. Understanding why they interact and why they move in certain ways is important. Interference helps to explain how waves react with each other, including phenomena such as how areas in a home theater can be made louder or quieter and how a clarinet works. The way that waves curve around objects and edges helps to explain why lower-pitched sounds travel the furthest because these sounds diffract more around obstacles in the way.

Conclusion

The world is full of waves—from the light waves emitted by the Sun to the sound waves produced during a thunderstorm. Radios receive waves that carry a signal that tells them what sound waves to produce. Cell phones send and receive microwaves to towers and satellites so that people can carry on phone conversations anywhere. Water waves erode the land and change the shape of shores around the world, whereas seismic waves topple buildings and crack open the ground. Understanding these types of events requires a person to know what a waves is, how it moves, and how it interacts with the world around it.

Waves use vibrations to transfer energy from one point to another. A wave that does not require a medium through which to travel is an electromagnetic wave. A wave that does need a medium through which to travel is a mechanical wave. Mechanical waves can travel as a transverse, longitudinal, or surface wave. For transverse waves, the particles of the medium vibrate in a direction that is perpendicular to the direction of the wave motion, like the seismic waves that are generated in an earthquake. The highest point of a transverse wave is called a crest, whereas the lowest is called a trough. The particles of a longitudinal wave vibrate in the same direction that the wave is traveling, such as with sound waves. The areas in which the particles of the medium are close together are compressions, and the areas in which the particles are spread out are rarefactions. Surface waves have a combination of transverse and longitudinal wave properties and move in a circular fashion. This phenomenon can be seen by an object floating on an ocean wave.

Many measurements can help describe and define a wave. The length of one cycle of a wave—crest and trough or compression and rarefaction—is the wavelength of the wave. The number of wavelengths that pass through a specific point in 1 second is the wave's frequency. The reciprocal of the frequency is the period of the wave—the time it takes for one wavelength to pass a point. Amplitude is a measurement of the greatest displacement for a transverse wave or the change in pressure of the air for a longitudinal sound wave. A wave's amplitude is a factor of how much energy the wave is carrying; waves that carry a large amount of energy have high amplitude. The velocity of a wave describes how far it can go in a given amount of time. For sound and light waves, all of these measurements help determine the brightness, loudness, color, or pitch produced by the wave.

Sound waves are produced when the particles of a medium—typically air—begin to vibrate and move closer together, forming a compression. As the energy that causes the vibration is transferred to new particles, the original particles slow down and spread out to form a rarefaction. Sound waves are often manipulated in many different ways to either dampen or enhance the waves. Sound-proofing involves blocking or absorbing sound waves to lower the amount that reaches a target, such as the noise barriers that block road noise from reaching nearby homes. Rooms and halls can be designed in manner that causes sound waves to travel further and to seem more robust through interference and reverberation.

One specific way that waves can interact with each other is through the Doppler effect when either the sound source or an observer is in motion. This effect causes the waves to become closer together—have a higher frequency—on one side of the source and further apart on the other. This change in frequency causes the pitch of a sound to appear to change as the source moves toward and then past an observer—higher as the object approaches and then lower as it moves away. Sound waves have many uses, including medical testing and treatment, the location of objects with sonar, and the cleaning of jewelry with ultrasonic waves.

Electromagnetic waves travel as an electric field vibrates and produces a vibrating magnetic field at a perpendicular angle. These fields reinforce each other and propagate a transverse wave that does not require a medium through which to travel. The electromagnetic spectrum consists of many different categories of waves that are classified by their uses and effects. These categories are radio waves, microwaves, infrared light, visible light, ultraviolet light, X-rays, and gamma rays. Radio waves have the longest wavelength, smallest frequency, and the least energy, whereas gamma rays have the shortest wavelength, highest frequency, and most energy. Lower-energy waves are considered nonionizing radiation because they do not have the energy required to remove an electron from the atoms with which they interact. Radio waves, microwaves, infrared light, visible light, and some types of ultraviolet light are nonionizing and thus do not mutate cells and cause cancer. Radio waves and microwaves are frequently used to transfer signals involved in communication, whereas infrared light is most commonly used to provide heat.

Ionizing radiation can damage DNA and cause mutations and cancer in human cells. The highest-energy ultraviolet light, X-rays, and gamma rays are all ionizing radiation; human exposure to these types of waves must be limited. Ultraviolet lamps are frequently used at crime scenes to detect traces of bodily fluids. X-rays are passed through a person's body to produce images of the bone, which absorbs the waves. Gamma rays can be used to target and kill cancer cells and bacteria in food that would cause it to spoil.

The small portion of the electromagnetic spectrum that is visible is responsible for all of the color in the world. From lowest to highest energy, the colors that make up visible light are as follows: red, orange, yellow, green, blue, indigo, and violet. When all colors are present in equal amounts, the light produced is white light. The dispersion of any type of visible light breaks the light into its component colors in the order of energy and wavelength. The color that an object appears is due to the colors of light that are reflected by the object because the reflected waves are the ones that reach an observer's eyes. Additive color mixing involves the addition of different colors of light to produce a specific color. When red, blue, and green lights are added, white light is produced; mixtures of these three primary additive colors can create any desired color. The color of most objects is determined through subtractive color mixing whereby different dyes and pigments are added to absorb particular colors of light. The three primary subtractive colors are magenta, cyan, and yellow; these colors produce black when all three are present.

When waves interact with their surrounding environment, they can do one of the following four things:

1. reflect from an object's surface,
2. be transmitted and refract as they change mediums,
3. interfere with each other, or
4. diffract as they move through an opening or around an obstacle.

When light rays reflect off an object, they can produce either a specular reflection or a diffuse reflection. The law of reflection states that the angle between the incident light ray and the normal—a line perpendicular to the surface at the point of impact—and the angle between the reflected light ray and the normal are always equal to each other. A specular reflection, or clear image, is created when light rays reflect off a smooth object in the same order and pattern as they were when they struck the object. A diffuse reflection is created when the reflected light rays are scattered in many directions from a rough surface.

There are three types of mirrors that create specular reflections—plane, concave, and convex. A plane mirror is a flat mirror that always creates an image that is virtual, upright, and the same size as the original object. An image is called virtual if the light rays appear to meet in a place in which they do not actually meet, such as the inside of a mirror. A concave mirror has a reflective surface that bends inward, causing the light rays that strike it to converge at a focal point some distance in front of the mirror, depending on how great the curvature of the mirror. A concave mirror can produce many different types of images, depending on where the object is located in front of the mirror. If the object is closer to the mirror than the focal point, it creates a virtual, upright, and magnified image. When the object is further away than the focal point, the image is real—that is, the light rays really cross and could be projected onto a screen—and inverted. The image can be either magnified or reduced in size; objects further away from the mirror are reduced in size. A convex mirror curves outward on its reflective side and always creates images that are virtual, upright, and reduced in size. Light rays can either be drawn in a ray diagram or calculations using the magnification and mirror equations can be done to determine the exact location of an image. Mirrors are used in telescopes, cameras, cars, and stores for security.

A wave bends as it travels from one medium to another because its speed changes in that material—the greater the change in speed, the greater the bend. The index of refraction of a material describes how much slower light waves move in that material versus through a vacuum. When light passes from one material to another, Snell's law uses the indices of refraction of the two materials and the angle of the incoming light ray to calculate the angle of the refracted light ray. Lenses are materials that refract light when they transmit the light rays. Most commonly, both sides of a lens are curved in the same way to create either a convex or a concave lens. Lenses also have focal points where the light rays converge or where they appear to diverge.

When the sides of a lens bulge outward, the lens is a convex, or converging, lens. When an object is placed between the focal point and the lens, it creates a virtual, upright, and magnified image. Objects placed beyond the focal point are real, inverted, and either reduced in size or magnified, depending on how far the object is placed from the focal point. Objects placed more than twice the focal length away from the lens are reduced in size, whereas those closer are magnified. A concave lens has sides that curve inward and always produces an image that is virtual, upright, and reduced in size. Ray diagrams and equations can be used to calculate the exact location of an image and to describe that image in terms of magnification and orientation. Lenses have many uses, including as magnifying glasses, in telescopes and cameras and in the correction of vision problems.

When two waves collide, they interfere with each other according to Huygens' principle of superposition. This principle provides an easier way to consider wave propagation by stating that each point in a wave front can be seen as the source of secondary waves that move away from it in all directions to continue the wave's motion. The principle also states that when two waves interact, the resulting wave has a displacement equal to the sum of the displacements of the original waves. The resulting idea of this principle is that two waves that add together in phase—with crest meeting crest and trough meeting trough—become a larger wave through constructive interference. Likewise, two waves that meet out of phase—with a crest interacting with a trough—become a smaller wave through destructive interference.

A standing wave pattern is created when a single wave interferes with itself by restricting the length of the medium available and by reflecting the wave back along the same path. A standing wave pattern has nodes that appear to be standing still and antinodes that oscillate between being the peak of a crest and the bottom of a trough. Standing waves are the basis of how wind and string instruments work as a standing wave pattern is created along the available medium to produce one specific note. Changing the length of the available medium changes the wavelength of the wave created and thus changes the note.

The final way in which waves interact with the world is through diffraction—the bending of a wave as it moves through an opening or around an obstacle. When diffraction occurs, the bent waves appear to be originating from the opening or from the edge of the obstacle because of the first statement of Huygens' principle of superposition and because of the way that the edges of the opening or obstacle block some of the secondary waves from adding together to form the new primary wave, thus changing the direction of the primary wave. The longer the wavelength of a wave, the more it diffracts; this principle is used to create rainbows with diffraction gratings—surfaces with ridges or grooves placed at regular intervals. Light rays diffract when they strike these obstacles; however, the different colors diffract at different rates due to their different wavelengths, thus causing the light to disperse into its component colors. Diffraction and interference together are used to create three-dimensional images called holograms.

Despite their apparent differences, sound and light have many things in common because they are both waves that carry energy. *Sound and Light* describes the similarities and differences based on the wave nature of these two important aspects of life. They both interact with the world as waves, although it is typically easier to witness the refraction and reflection of light waves as opposed to sound waves. Both light and sound waves have many uses, from medical to entertainment. The reader should gain a better understanding of these uses based on the knowledge gained from the information in this book.

SI Units and Conversions

UNIT	QUANTITY	SYMBOL	CONVERSION
Base units			
meter	length	m	1 m = 3.2808 feet
kilogram	mass	kg	1 kg = 2.205 pounds
second	time	s	
ampere	electric current	A	
kelvin	thermodynamic temperature	K	1 K = 1°C = 1.8°F
candela	luminous intensity		
mole	amount of substance	d mol	
Supplementary Units			
radian	plane angle	rad	π / 2 rad = 90°
steradian	solid angle	sr	
Derived Units			
coulomb	quantity of electricity	C	
cubic meter	volume	m^3	1 m^3 = 1.308 $yards^3$
farad	capacitance	F	
henry	inductance	H	
hertz	frequency	Hz	
joule	energy	J	1 J = 0.2389 calories
kilogram per cubic meter	density	$kg\ m^{-3}$	1 $kg\ m^{-3}$ = 0.0624 lb. ft^{-3}
lumen	luminous flux	lm	
lux	illuminance	lx	
meter per second	speed	$m\ s^{-1}$	1 $m\ s^{-1}$ = 3.281 $ft\ s^{-1}$

UNIT	QUANTITY	SYMBOL	CONVERSION
meter per second squared	acceleration	$m\ s^{-2}$	
mole per cubic meter	concentration	$mol\ m^{-3}$	
newton	force	N	1 N = 7.218 lb. force
ohm	electric resistance	Ω	
pascal	pressure	Pa	$1\ Pa = \dfrac{0.145\ lb}{in^{-2}}$
radian per second	angular velocity	$rad\ s^{-1}$	
radian per second squared	angular acceleration	$rad\ s^{-2}$	
square meter	area	m^2	$1\ m^2 = 1.196\ yards^2$
tesla	magnetic flux density	T	
volt	electromotive force	V	
watt	power	W	$1W = 3.412\ Btu\ h^{-1}$
weber	magnetic flux	Wb	

PREFIXES USED WITH SI UNITS		
PREFIX	SYMBOL	VALUE
atto	a	10^{-18}
femto	f	10^{-15}
pico	p	10^{-12}
nano	n	10^{-9}
micro		10^{-6}
milli	m	10^{-3}
centi	c	10^{-2}
deci	d	10^{-1}
deca	da	10
hecto	h	10^{2}
kilo	k	10^{3}
mega	M	10^{6}
giga	G	10^{9}
tera	T	10^{12}

PHYSICS PRINCIPLES: SOUND AND LIGHT

The following serves as a reference to provide additional information on important topics and further understanding of the material covered in this book. It includes brief explanations of the laws, theories, and major concepts covered in this book and lists the chapter in which the topic is first introduced, although other chapters may also include the topic. Not all chapters are listed here because they may not introduce a major theory or concept.

ELECTROMAGNETISM (CHAPTER 2)
Electromagnetism is one of the four fundamental forces of nature; the other three forces are gravity, weak nuclear force, and strong nuclear force. Both the weak and strong nuclear forces are only felt within the atom, thus gravity and electromagnetism are responsible for all of the forces experienced in everyday life. Electromagnetism is the force that causes attraction and repulsion between charged particles and between magnets. When these forces occur on a large scale, such as when one person pushes another, this interaction still occurs as a result of electromagnetism from the interactions of the electrons and protons within the atoms that make up each person. Electromagnetism first became widely recognized in 1820 when Danish physicist Hans Christian Ørsted (1777–1851) noticed that the needle of a compass was deflected when placed near a current carrying wire. Further research found that electrical current created a magnetic field that was perpendicular to the electrical path. Electromagnetic theory has four main points: (1) electric charges attract or repel one another, (2) magnetic poles attract or repel one another, (3) an electric current creates a magnetic field, and (4) a magnetic field creates an electrical current in a wire when there is relative motion between the two. Scottish physicist James Clerk Maxwell (1831–79) was responsible for unifying these interactions and for showing that they are all caused by the same force—electromagnetism. This development eventually led to the discovery that light is an electromagnetic wave made up of an electric and a magnetic field.

DUAL NATURE OF LIGHT (CHAPTER 3)

The dual nature of light states that light behaves as both a particle and a wave. Research spanning at least two centuries solidified and proved this idea. Until the 19th century, physicists debated whether light was a wave or a particle. The first experimental proof was found in the early 19th century when British physicist Thomas Young (1773–1829) performed his double-slit experiment. In his experiment, Young shined light on a surface that had two narrow slits cut into it and projected the light passing through the slits onto a screen. The light passing through the slits produced evenly spaced bright and dark bands of color. Young discovered that the bright and dark stripes were caused by constructive and destructive interference of the light waves as these waves diffracted through the opening. Scottish physicist James Clerk Maxwell (1831–79), who unified electromagnetism, strengthened the wave theory of light with his mathematical proof that light behaves as an electromagnetic wave. Thus, scientists accepted the wave nature of light as the only answer throughout the 19th century.

It was not until 1905 that the particle theory of light was revisited. German physicist Albert Einstein (1879–1955) calculated that light was actually a particle, or photon; his calculation helped to explain the photoelectric effect. Einstein explained that if light were a stream of particles, it would stand to reason that when the particles strike a metal, electrons might be emitted from the collisions between the incident (or incoming) particles and the atoms of the metal. The dual nature of light has been extended to encompass all types of matter; therefore, everything is now known to have a dual wave/particle nature. These concepts became key ideas in the development of quantum mechanics.

LAW OF REFLECTION (CHAPTER 5)

Although the law of reflection may have been known since ancient times, the first known publication of this law was in 1637 when French philosopher René Descartes (1596–1650) published his essay on optics. The law of reflection states that when light is reflected off a surface, the angle of incidence is equal to the angle of reflection. The angle of incidence is the angle between the incoming light ray before reflection and the normal—a line perpendicular to the surface at the point the light ray strikes. The angle of reflection is the angle between the light ray after reflection and the normal. This law explains why clear images are created from smooth surfaces but not from rough surfaces. When a man stands in front of a mirror, millions of light rays bounce off his face. According to the law of reflection, all light rays that strike a smooth surface, like a mirror, have the same angle of reflection because the normal for each light ray has the exact same orientation. Thus, a clear image is formed when all of the light rays reflect in the same pattern. Light rays that strike a rough surface, like a wall, do not form a clear image because they bounce off the surface in all different directions (i.e., no pattern is formed at all). The normal for each light ray that strikes a rough surface is orientated differently based on the configuration of the surface at the exact location where it strikes. The light rays do still reflect though, which is why sometimes reflections off brightly colored objects are slightly visible. The law of reflection explains how, why, and where images are seen when an observer looks at a smooth surface.

SNELL'S LAW (CHAPTER 6)

When a light ray refracts as it moves from one medium to another, Snell's law can be applied to show the relationships between the indices of refraction for the two materials, the angle at which the incoming light ray strikes the border between the mediums, and the angle at which the refracted ray leaves the border. The equation is as follows:

$$n_i \sin \theta_i = n_r \sin \theta_r ,$$

where n is the index of refraction, subscript i indicates that the value is for the incident (or incoming) light ray, and subscript r indicates that the measurement describes the refracted light ray.

All angles are measured between the light ray and the normal at the surface where the light ray strikes. This law shows that the greater the difference between the indices of refraction for the materials, the greater the difference in their angles. If a wave moves from a lower index of refraction to a higher index of refraction—the wave speed decreases—the wave bends toward the normal. The opposite is also true. If light moves from a higher to a lower index of refraction—the wave increases speed—the wave bends away from the normal.

The origins of this law and its name are contested. This law is also sometimes called the law of refraction, the Snell-Descartes law, or Descartes law. Muslim physicist Ibn Sahl (940–1000) was the first to provide an accurate description of this law, which he published 984. In 1921, Dutch mathematician Willebrord Snel (1580–1626) derived another version of the law but never published it. In 1637, French philosopher René Descartes (1596–1650) published the law in his essay on optics, although some accused him of copying Snel's work. Even more scientists discovered or calculated this law, although they were not the first to do so or destined to ever receive credit in the law's name. Despite its complicated history, Snell's law allows for a mathematical explanation for the bending of light rays as they move from one medium to another.

HUYGENS' PRINCIPLE OF SUPERPOSITION (CHAPTER 7)

Huygens' principle of superposition has two main points. First, every point on a moving wave front can be thought of as producing secondary waves that spread in all directions and sum together to make the new wave front of the wave. Thus, the source of a wave always appears to be changing to the area just behind the wave front. Second, when two waves collide, the resulting wave is the sum of the displacement—or amplitude—of the two original waves. This principle helps to explain how light waves interfere with each other to produce light and dark stripes on a screen when they pass through two slits as in Young's double-slit experiment. At every point within the slit, the wave front is producing waves in a circular pattern. These waves interfere with the waves created adjacent to them, creating bright spots when they interfere constructively and dark spots when they interfere destructively. The principle helps explain diffraction because the points just inside of the edge of an opening, or at the end of an obstacle, are still producing waves in all directions, causing the overall wave to seem to spread out or bend.

The principle also helps to explain refraction when waves move from one medium to another. As the wave approaches the boundary between two mediums, the points closest to the boundary create secondary waves that cross the border first while other points on the wave front are still creating waves in the original medium. The differences in speed from one end of the wave to another causes the wave to bend, just as when a lawnmower goes from the sidewalk onto the grass. The new surface causes those wheels in contact with it to slow, changing the trajectory of the lawnmower until all tires are on the same surface. This principle is vital to understanding diffraction, refraction, and interference.

GLOSSARY

AMPLITUDE   A measurement of the maximum displacement of a wave from its rest position.

ANTINODE   The part of a standing wave that is continuously moving from crest to trough, or compression to rarefaction, because of constructive interference.

BIG BANG THEORY   The theory that attributes the creation of the universe to an event similar to an explosion. The expansion of the universe, cosmic background radiation, and the laws of physics support this theory.

COMPRESSIONS   The portions of a longitudinal wave where the particles of the medium are closest together.

CONCAVE LENS   A lens with one or more sides that are curved inward. This type of lens is called a diverging lens because it causes light rays to spread out when refracted.

CONCAVE MIRROR   A mirror with a reflective side that is curved inward. This type of mirror is called a converging mirror because after reflection, the light rays come together.

CONSTRUCTIVE INTERFERENCE   Interference that occurs when two waves that meet primarily in phase—crest to crest or trough to trough—interact with each other to produce a wave of greater amplitude.

CONVEX LENS   A lens with one or more sides that are curved outward. This type of lens is called a converging lens because it causes light rays to come together when refracted.

CONVEX MIRROR   A mirror with a reflective side that is curved outward. This type of mirror is called a diverging mirror because after reflection, the light rays spread out.

CREST   The point of highest, positive amplitude on a transverse wave.

DECIBELS   The unit of measurement for the intensity, or power, of sound. The scale on which decibels are measured is logarithmic and gives a value relative to a specific reference level. A decibel is one-tenth of a bel.

DESTRUCTIVE INTERFERENCE   Interference that occurs when two waves that meet primarily out of phase—crest to trough—interact with each other to produce a wave of lesser amplitude.

DIFFRACTION The bending of waves as they pass through an opening or around an obstacle.

DIFFUSE REFLECTION The reflection of light off a rough surface that does not produce a clear image.

DISPERSION When light is broken down into the colors contained within it because of the differences in the wavelength of each color.

DOPPLER EFFECT The change in a wave's frequency caused by the relative motion between the wave source and an observer. This is sometimes called *Doppler shift*.

ELECTROMAGNETIC WAVES A wave that consists of an electric field and a magnetic field oscillating perpendicularly to each other. This type of wave does not require a medium through which to travel.

FREQUENCY The number of wavelengths that pass a given point in 1 second. Frequency is measured in hertz (Hz).

FRICTION The resistance to relative motion on the surfaces of two objects in contact with each other.

INDEX OF REFRACTION The ratio of the speed of light in a vacuum to the speed of light in a given medium. This measurement describes how slowly light moves through a medium.

INFRASOUND A sound wave below the typical threshold of human hearing, 20 hertz.

IONIZING RADIATION Radiation that has enough energy to remove an electron from an atom.

LAW OF REFLECTION A law that states that when a wave strikes a surface, the angle of incidence (the angle between the incoming ray and the normal) equals the angle of reflection (the angle between the reflected ray and the normal).

LONGITUDINAL WAVES A wave in which the particles vibrate in the same direction as the wave travels.

LUMINOUS The property of generating and emitting electromagnetic radiation.

MECHANICAL WAVES Waves that require a medium through which to travel.

MEDIUM A physical substance through which a wave can travel.

NODES   The areas in a standing wave pattern that do not appear to move because of destructive interference.

NONIONIZING RADIATION   Radiation that does not have enough energy to remove electrons from atoms.

NORMAL   A line that is perpendicular to a surface at a specific point.

OPTICAL DENSITY   The ease with which light travels through a substance because of how quickly the particles of the substance absorb and reemit electromagnetic waves.

PERIOD   A measurement of how long it takes for one wavelength to pass a given point. Period is measured in seconds (s).

PHOTOELECTRIC EFFECT   The emission of electrons from a metal when it is struck by light. This effect was used to prove the particle nature of light.

PHOTON   A particle with zero mass and no electric charge that carries a fixed amount of electromagnetic energy.

PITCH   The way in which the brain interprets the frequency of a sound wave. A sound wave with a high frequency will be high pitched, whereas a sound with low frequency will be low pitched.

PLANE MIRROR   A mirror with a reflective side that is perfectly flat.

PRIMARY ADDITIVE COLORS   The three colors of light—red, blue, and green—that can form any other color of light by the addition of colors. Together these three colors produce white.

PRIMARY SUBTRACTIVE COLORS   The three colors of dyes or pigments—red, cyan, and magenta—through which any color can be produced by absorbing different colors. Together these three colors produce black.

RAREFACTIONS   The portions of a longitudinal wave where the particles of the medium are the most spread out.

REAL IMAGE   An image formed when light rays converge at a point. This type of image can be projected onto a screen.

REFLECTION   When waves bounce off a surface.

REFRACTION The bending of waves as they pass from one medium to another.

RELATIVE VELOCITY The velocity of an object with respect to another object used as a frame of reference.

REVERBERATION The continuation of a sound caused by the reflection of the sound waves.

SNELL'S LAW An equation that states that when a light ray passes from one medium to another, the index of refraction of the first medium multiplied by the sine of the angle of incidence is equal to the index of refraction of the second medium multiplied by the sine of the angle of refraction. This law is also known as the law of refraction, Descartes' Law, and the Snell-Descartes' Law.

SPECULAR REFLECTION The reflection of light off a smooth surface, which produces a clear image because of the orderly reflection of the light waves.

STANDING WAVES A wave pattern that can be produced when the medium of a mechanical wave is restricted in length where parts of the wave appear to be motionless.

SURFACE WAVES A wave that combines properties of transverse and longitudinal waves, in which the particles of the medium move in a circular motion.

TOTAL INTERNAL REFLECTION A type of reflection in which a light ray traveling in an optically dense material strikes the boundary between mediums at an angle greater than the critical angle, causing the angle of refraction to be greater than 90° and completely reflecting the light ray back into the original medium.

TRANSVERSE WAVES A wave in which the particles of the medium vibrate in a direction perpendicular to the direction in which the wave travels.

TROUGH The point of lowest, negative amplitude on a transverse wave.

ULTRASOUND A sound above the typical range of human hearing, 20,000 hertz.

VELOCITY A measurement of the time it takes an object to move a distance in a specific direction. Velocity is measured in meters per second (m/s).

VIRTUAL IMAGE An image formed when light rays diverge where the light rays do not meet where they appear to do so.

WAVELENGTH The length of one full cycle of a wave, including a crest and a trough or a compression and rarefaction. Wavelength is measured in meters (m).

WHITE LIGHT Light that appears colorless but contains all of the colors of visible light.

FURTHER RESOURCES

Print and Internet

Barron, Michael. *Auditorium Acoustics and Architectural Design*. London: E & FN Spon, 1993. A book that describes how the interference of sound waves and acoustic principles are used when designing auditoriums.

Boyle, W.S. "Light-Wave Communications." *Scientific American*, October 6, 2009. Available online. URL: www.scientificamerican.com/article. cfm?id=light-wave-communications. Accessed November 9, 2010. The article is an online reprint of an article that was originally published in August 1977 that describes the development of fiber optic technology.

Cardis, Elisabeth. "Brain Tumour Risk in Relation to Mobile Telephone Use: Results of the INTERPHONE International Case-Control Study." *International Journal of Epidemiology* 39.3 (June 2010): 675–694. Available online. URL: ije.oxfordjournals.org/content/39/3/675.full. Accessed October 5, 2010. A paper that describes an international study done on the possible relationship between cell phone usage and brain tumors and concludes that no such relationship exists.

Cunningham, Andrew, and Bruce Thomas. "Target Motion Analysis Visualisation." 2005 Asia Pacific Symposium on Information Visualisation, Sydney, Australia, Vol. 45. Available online. URL: www.acs.org.au/documents/public/crpit/CRPITV45Cunningham .pdf. Accessed September 16, 2010. This paper presents research done on how target motion analysis—particularly the use of passive sonar—can be improved and explains how these types of systems are used.

Ekspong, Gösta. "The Dual Nature of Light as Reflected in the Nobel Archives." December 2, 1999. Available online. URL: nobelprize. org/nobel_prizes/physics/articles/ekspong/. Accessed September 28, 2010. An article explaining the research that lead to the understanding of the dual nature of light and the Noble Prizes that were awarded for this research.

Enoch, Jay M. "History of Mirrors Dating Back 8000 Years." *Optometry and Vision Science* 83.10 (October 2006): 775–781. Available online. URL: journals.lww.com/optvissci/Fulltext/2006/10000/History_of_ Mirrors_Dating_Back_8000_Years_.17.aspx. Accessed October 12, 2010. This article describes how mirrors have been made and used throughout history and explains their impact on society.

Flowers, Charles. *Instability Rules: The Ten Most Amazing Ideas of Modern Science*. New York: John Wiley & Sons, Inc., 2002. This publication presents an interesting and easily understood description of ten important principles of modern science and their impact.

Freeman, Michael. *Mastering Color Digital Photography*. New York: Lark Books, 2006. This book discusses how color relates to digital photography, including how color is perceived, and explains color theory.

Graham, Sarah. "Sound Waves Chill in New Freezer Design." *Scientific American*, December 4, 2002. Available online. URL: www.scientific american.com/article.cfm?id=sound-waves-chill-in-new. Accessed November 8, 2010. An article that explains new research done in the use of sound waves, and the energy that they carry, to power freezers in the future.

Horváth, Gábor, and Dezsö Varjú. "Geometric Optical Investigation of the Underwater Visual Field of Aerial Animals." *Mathematical Biosciences* 102 (1990): 1–19. Available online. URL: arago.elte.hu/old/PUBLICATIONS/CIKKEK/ANGOL/underwater-visual-field-of-aerial-animals_MBS.pdf. Accessed October 20, 2010. This paper discusses research done on the consequences of refraction on the visual field of aerial creatures hunting for prey underwater.

Johnson, George. *The Ten Most Beautiful Experiments*. New York: Alferd A. Knopf, 2008. The author describes and explains ten of the most important and fascinating experiments ever conducted.

Kick, Winston E. *Lasers & Holography: An Introduction to Coherent Optics*. Mineola, NY: Dover Publications, 1981. The author explains what holograms are and how they use the diffraction of light to create a three-dimensional image.

Kindig, Steve. "Room Acoustics." May 4, 2010. Available online. URL: www.crutchfield.com/learn/learningcenter/home/speakers_roomacoustics.html. Accessed September 14, 2010. An article that describes how sound waves are controlled through acoustics to produce a good sound when setting up for a home theater system.

Merola, Joseph S. "Why Isn't the Dual Wave/Particle Nature of the Quantum Mechanical World Present in the Macroscopic World (Say, for a Basketball)?" *Scientific American*, February 16, 1998. Available online. URL: www.scientificamerican.com/article.cfm?id=why-isnt-the-dual-wavepar. Accessed November 9, 2010. This article quickly and simply explains why the dual wave/particle nature of the world is not apparent in most cases.

Minkel, J. R. "Light Bent the Wrong Way—Can an Invisibility Cloak Be Far Behind?" *Scientific American*, August 12, 2008. Available online. URL: www.scientificamerican.com/blog/post.cfm?id=light-bent-the-wrong-waycan-an-invi-2008-08-12. Accessed November 9, 2010. This short article describes new materials, called *metamaterials*, that can bend light backward.

Oates, Chris. "How Were the Speed of Sound and the Speed of Light Determined and Measured?" *Scientific American*, June 9, 2003. Available online. URL: www.scientificamerican.com/article.cfm?id=how-were-the-speed-of-sou. Accessed November 8, 2010. The author responds to a question about how the speeds of light and sound were first measured.

Perkowitz, Sidney. *Empire of Light: A History of Discovery in Science and Art*. New York: Henry Holt and Company, 1996. This book describes the way the understanding of light has developed over time and how light is used, particularly in terms of art.

Saeta, Peter N. "What Is the Physical Process by which a Mirror Reflects Light Rays?" *Scientific American*. October 21, 1999. Available online. URL: www.scientificamerican.com/article.cfm?id=what-is-the-physical-proc. Accessed November 9, 2010. The author explains what happens on the atomic level when light reflects off a surface.

Simon, Caroline J., Damian E. Dupuy, and William W. May-Smith. "Microwave Ablation: Principles and Applications." *RadioGraphics* 25 (October 2005): S69–S63. Available online. URL: radiographics.rsna.org/content/25/suppl_1/S69.abstract. Accessed September 30, 2010. This article discusses the use of microwaves to kill cancer tumors by placing an antenna directly into the tumor and allowing it to release electromagnetic radiation.

Woo, Joseph. "A Short History of the Development of Ultrasound in Obstetrics and Gynecology." Available online. URL: www.ob-ultrasound.net/history1.html. Accessed September 16, 2010. An article that details the development of ultrasound and its current uses today in obstetrics and gynecology.

Web Sites

HyperPhysics. Available online. URL: hyperphysics.phy-astr.gsu.edu/hbase/hph.html. Accessed September 26, 2010. This Web site, maintained by the Department of Physics and Astronomy at Georgia

State University, covers a multitude of physics topics in a straightforward and easy-to-understand manner.

NASA: For Students. Available online. URL: www.nasa.gov/audience/forstudents/index.html. Accessed September 28, 2010. This Web site contains a great deal of information, including a description of the electromagnetic spectrum, geared toward students.

National Radio Astronomy Observatory. Available online. URL: www.nrao.edu. Accessed September 26, 2010. A Web site that describes and explains radio astronomy.

INDEX